DATE DUE

JUN 2 1 2007	
JUL 0 5 2007	
SEP 2 6 2007	
OCT 1 3 2007	
NOV 2 1 2007	
JUL 2 1 2008	

BRODART.   Cat. No. 23-221

MAMARAMA

MAMARAMA

A Memoir of Sex, Kids, and Rock 'n' Roll

Evelyn McDonnell

Da Capo

LIFE
LONG

Da Capo Lifelong
A Member of the Perseus Books Group

A list of credits/permissions can be found on page 249.

Many of the designations used by manufacturers and sellers to distinguish their products are claimed as trademarks. Where those designations appear in this book and Da Capo Press was aware of a trademark claim, the designations have been printed in initial capital letters.

Copyright © 2007 by Evelyn McDonnell

Designed by Timm Bryson
Set in 11-point Electra by the Perseus Books Group

Cataloging-in-Publication data for this book is available from the Library of Congress.

First Da Capo Press edition 2007
ISBN-13: 978-0-7382-1054-4
ISBN-10: 0-7382-1054-4

Published by Da Capo Press
A Member of the Perseus Books Group
www.dacapopress.com

Da Capo Press books are available at special discounts for bulk purchases in the U.S. by corporations, institutions, and other organizations. For more information, please contact the Special Markets Department at the Perseus Books Group, 11 Cambridge Center, Cambridge, MA 02142, or call (800) 255-1514 or (617) 252-5298, or email special.markets@perseusbooks.com.

10 9 8 7 6 5 4 3 2 1

To Mom, Mama, and mothers.

And to Karlie, Kenda, and Cole.

Contents

	Preface: Flipping the Script	ix
1	Dreaming Is Free	1
2	Queens of Noise	13
3	Set It Off	23
4	New York Woman	35
5	No Martyrs	55
6	The Gay '90s	67
7	Noise Equals Life	81
8	Love Will Tear Us Apart	97
9	Wild Things	119
10	Kick Out the Jams, Mothers	137

11	Welcome to Miami	155
12	Broken Water	169
13	Bringing Up Baby	185
14	Mamarama	201
15	About a Boy (and Girls)	219
16	Dig the New Breeders	235
	Acknowledgments	247
	Credits	249

Preface: Flipping the Script

The day I started writing this book was my son's first day at preschool.

Or should I write, my son's first day at preschool was the day I started writing this book?

It's a trick question, I admit, one that carries its own rhetorical subtext: Do words, reordered, reflect priorities or create false dichotomies? Back in the early '90s, when I was a twenty-whatever culture critic who found meanings of life in obscure songs and freshly hatched poetry, I was attached to a similar identity riddle, written by Jean Smith of the Vancouver-based punk performance duo Mecca Normal: "A man might think she's singing while she braids her hair. She is not. She braids her hair while she sings." The lyric flipped a literary cliché—a male author's view of an objectified woman—on its ass. Smith was speaking for a legion of us women who were forging our identities in the wake of the

'80s antifemale backlash. We were the girls who braided their hair as they sang. (Frankly, I did neither well.) Looks were secondary to expression; grooming was something my generation/posse/clique/movement did while we created. But we did groom. We weren't the unshaven women's libbers of '70s yore. Well, actually, I didn't shave back then, but I did wear lipstick, and miniskirts, and fishnet stockings.

It was the early '90s, when direct activism, identity politics, hip-hop, and grunge were driving forces of the dawn of the Clinton era. We were a new breed of woman whom pundits, including some in our own ranks, struggled to name: postfeminists, woman-ists, Riot Grrrls, pro-sex feminists, do-me feminists (a name obviously thought up by a men's magazine), third-wave feminists, lipstick lesbians, bitches with attitudes. We were students of, and rebels against, women's herstory. Our ideas sometimes clashed wildly. One fanzine brilliantly came up with the term *hypocrobrat* to describe our delicate balancing act: being sexy without being sexist. We walked bare-breasted down Fifth Avenue with "slut" written across our stomachs. We wore gorilla/guerrilla masks and protested male-dominated art and civic institutions. We rewrote billboards, published fanzines, grabbed mikes, scratched records, smashed drums.

But there was one thing few of us did: have children.

I remember a list that was passed around among us female rock critics, who were staging our own minicollectivization: "10 reasons why a book is better than a baby." I don't remember the specific antibreeding digs, but the point was clear: We should make something of our own lives first, before we start making other lives. It was a lesson that my mom, a gifted teacher who didn't want me to make the same sacrifices for family that she had, had been telling me for years. Still, even back then, the list irritated me: Why did one goal have to be pitted against the other?

Ever since I can remember, I've wanted to write. I've also wanted to have children, but that was a far less conscious desire than the one to be a writer—maybe because it seemed inevitable, as if it went without saying. Maybe because (or so I thought) the goal of parenting (socially accepted, even expected) doesn't need to be pronounced and pursued with the same focus and ferocity as that of writing (uncertain and suspiciously asocial). Or maybe because I just wanted to be a writer more than I wanted to be a mother.

One was never meant to preclude the other. One shouldn't preclude the other. One didn't preclude the other. In fact, on a beautiful January morning, the start of a new year and early in the beginning of a new decade of my life, the two desires colluded to start me down a middle passage, one as full of unorthodox choices, bad turns, and hidden delights as I've tried to make my life so far.

My son, Cole, walked the one and a half blocks to his Miami Beach Montessori preschool. Parents and grandparents nervously hovered by his side. In one hand, he clutched a mangled family of small red flowers he had picked from the neighbor's bushes, as he did every time we headed east: At twenty-one months, he was already a little man, conquering nature, taking a piece of home with him wherever he went. In the other hand, he gripped the remains of a cookie. Cole was happy, until we got outside the school building and he sensed his fate. My towheaded masterpiece had only barely begun the art/burden of mastering language; still, rarely has the word "no" been pronounced with such precise authority.

But inside, when he saw all the toys, when he saw the picture of his cat and dog, which Mama had brought as his "family portrait," hanging on the wall, when his teacher sat him down at the little table across from a raven-haired beauty named Priscilla and offered him some goldfish crackers if he would just unclutch his flowers, then the most definitive no became the most affirmative yes. Cole opened his fist and dropped the crumpled scarlet petals into his teacher's hand, nodded and pronounced every aspirant and sibilant of that "y-e-s," and began a new phase of his life too, the one in which his world would begin to expand beyond mama, papa, half-sisters, and pets; in which he would begin the great, and not-so-great, American socialization process (or, as his father says, become indoctrinated into the middle class); in which he would learn to be as stubbornly independent as his family clans, to carry his own backpack.

I walked home and into my office, turned on the computer, and sat down. With three hours of Cole-free writing time ahead of me, I finally started, well, not the great American novel, but a story in part peculiarly mine. It's also the story of many women I know, whose paths mine has converged with and diverged from over the years. And it's the story of the cultural pioneers who inspired us, the women who rested Stratocasters on pregnant bellies and pushed prams past beatnik deadbeats. Ultimately, it's a story, I think, replete with the kinds of experiences shared by thousands of women (men, too) who have spent the first few decades of their lives pursuing one dream, treading (or sometimes being trodden upon) along the road less traveled, plumbing the byways of the American music underground or writing romance novels in Europe. Then, one day, they find themselves moved to their souls by the fact that, at eighteen months, their child has learned the itsy-bitsy spider song.

At forty years old, I found more than just the pride and joy that connects me with billions of parents across millennia and continents. I also found my voice. It's the same voice with which I championed New Zealand bands ("underground rock from down under"), cheered on lady MCs ("go, Yo Yo!"), discovered Nuyorican poets, praised PJ Harvey's voluptuous mouth, and got confessional in fanzines. I was right: The book-versus-baby list was stupid. As the cliché goes, parenting is the hardest job (for an extra grind, try step-parenting). But it'll straighten your perspective right out. What else could a writer ask for?

Almost two years into the job, as I began to find my equilibrium in the roiling sea of emotions, as Cole howled his way into his second day of preschool and I slinked guiltily home to my laptop, I decided that the adage–cum–TV commercial that had become my aughties mantra is both right and wrong: A baby changes everything. Except your self.

1

Dreaming Is Free

∾ ∾ ∾

I would have taken a bullet for Michael.

That was the fantasy: I'm in Los Angeles, land of my birth and of Michael Jackson's superstardom. Usually, the setting is an amusement park (as a seven-year-old who had been transplanted to a Midwestern town, I pictured California as one big family fun zone). With a towering steel-and-wood roller-coaster as a mountain-range backdrop, the pint-sized lead singer of the Jackson 5 is spreading his love on his followers. I'm there (to comfort him, wrap my world of dreams around him, I'm so glad that I found him), at the front of the crowd, awaiting his benediction—a word, a glance, an autograph.

Michael and I are mere feet apart when I see the man with the gun. Menacing. Jealous. A hater.

"No!" I scream, and the next few seconds pass in slow motion.

I leap in front of Michael as the muzzle flashes . . . The bullet lodges in my shoulder, perilously close to my heart. . . . Guards tackle the assassin, and Michael rushes to my side.

"You saved my life," he says, gently, sadly, tenderly.

"I love you," I whisper.

We both cry.

Assassination fascination: I suppose it's what happens when you were born less than a year after John F. Kennedy was killed, when the slayings of Martin Luther King Jr., Robert Kennedy, and Malcolm X punctuated your toddler years like so many cosmic time-outs. I imagine it's a shared trait of "my generation," that is, no generation—we of that age group that's too squirrelly for the yuppies and too old-school for the slackers. Who knows, maybe news of the gunman at the Rolling Stones' '69 Altamont concert had penetrated my grade-school consciousness. I always was a bit of a pop culture junkie.

My first crush was a cartoon—a cartoon who was a child prodigy, who became the King of Pop, who devolved into a surgical composite of our culture's psychic breakdown. In 1971 *The Jackson 5ive*, a series produced by animation kings Rankin-Bass, made being music stars look like the Great American Adventure. The five brothers carried on the tradition of *The Monkees*, the Beatles in *A Hard Day's Night*, and Our Gang in *Little Rascals*. Only the Jacksons were our age, sort of. (Being a cartoon made them seem younger than they were.) I was born the year the Beatles played *The Ed Sullivan Show*; the Monkees were more my older brother's cup of tea. But musicians beamed every Saturday morning onto the TV screen in my Midwestern ranch-house living room made rock and roll seem like the Jetsons' space home or the Flintstones' stone age: a domesticated fantasy realm.

My brother has confessed that around the same time I was obsessing about Michael's fancy footwork, fuzzy Afro, and angel voice, he fell for Speed Racer's limpid eyes. Brett, two years older and cerebrally light years ahead of me, was my partner in pop-cultural immersion. Cartoons helped us imagine a miscegenated, bisexual future. But how were we, as adults, supposed to manage real-life relationships when we got our start with the perennial happy endings of Technicolor, bubble-edged creations?

Some three decades later, the ironies of my prepubescent imagination are abundantly clear. These days, Michael Jackson gets arrested for allegedly acting out fantasies somewhat different from my own, with little boys, not little girls. Apparently, life in the Jackson 5 was not quite the fantastic adventure depicted in cartoons.

But the '70s were an age of innocence. I wanted not merely to meet Michael, become his girlfriend, and save him—Did I somehow know he needed rescuing? Was it, in fact, obvious?—I wanted, of course, to be him. A rock star. A singing, dancing world traveler. A being whose divine gift lifted him above the dull, daily duties of life (homework, jobs, dishes, bills).

I wonder if Michael wishes he had had my relatively normal, safe, happy, if daydream-obsessed, childhood. Would he star in this role-play movie, trade places with not necessarily me, but someone like me? Someone not on a crash course for obliteration by the dream/hit factory, his very face erased.

I'm not sure those dreams did either of us any good.

But we'll always have the music.

Jackson 5 Greatest Hits. All music obsessives ask each other, What was your first album? That was mine. Plus, I owned a 45 of "Ben," Michael's love song to a rat. Seven-inch vinyl was where it was at when I was growing up in a small Wisconsin city. We heard the songs played by WLS in Chicago on our transistor radios, saved our allowances, rode our bikes to K-Mart, and brought home the hits. Though record collecting now seems to have become the ultimate nerdy fanboy domain, it was we girls who traded 45s while boys fretted over baseball cards.

A testament to the mentality of the collector, I still own that dog-eared album. On the cover, Michael looks nothing like the specter that haunts tabloid television. His image is positively Afrocentric in that groovy '70s way: big hair, nose, lips, collar. He's wearing a choker, and his colorful shirt is open. Michael doesn't look like an adult, but he's no kid either.

The joy, the glee, the abandon, the excitement are all in his voice. The Beatles were great, yeah, but sometimes I think pop music truly peaked later, with the bubblegum soul of the Jackson 5. John, Paul, George, and Ringo would have been inspiration-impaired without Motown, the Sound of Young America. And in Michael, Motown head Berry Gordy found what he had always been looking for: an old soul with a young voice.

Pop music is Peter Pan, the Pied Piper. It's Ponce de Leon's fountain of youth bottled and sold worldwide or spritzed into the air for free. Hear a song you loved as a child three decades later, and you're young again. Connect with a current hit, even as a middle-aged geezer, and you've tapped into the secret society of youth culture.

I bought into the dream factory big time, and it still levies a tithe on my soul. I've just always loved music. Dancing on a coffee table at my parents' cocktail parties, I would entertain the guests by singing all the parts on the *Hair* and *Jesus Christ Superstar* soundtracks. The Beatles—all four of them; why choose?—were among my earliest adolescent crushes. Punk rock saved my bored, zit-faced teenage life and taught me to screech, "Oh bondage, up yours." Funk taught me to dance, hip-hop showed me the news, and electronica transported me. Along the way, I decided to write about it all.

Some people are born musicians. I was born a listener. My first concert memories are of Dave Brubeck playing the slinky chords of "Take 5" by the Lake Michigan shore every year at Milwaukee's outdoor beer bacchanal, Summerfest. My family's table would be full of empty cups and fried-food containers, and my parents would be in front of the stage swing dancing. At night's end, Brett and I would pile into the back of the station wagon and sleep on the hour-and-a-half ride home down a quiet highway. Getting a DUI wasn't a suburban bête noire in those days, and I always felt safe in our Chevy cocoon, watching the star-filled country sky out the back window.

Occasionally, Dad would take out one of his classical records and ensconce himself in our living room, where he would sink deep into the strings. Usually, this was late at night, and he would be in some kind of mood. Sometimes, we'd have to ask him to put the headphones on, but even so, he would shout along to some rousing section, causing the rest of us to giggle. Brett adopted similar habits when he hit adolescence, but his headphone affairs were with the Doors, Bruce Springsteen, and the Clash.

Suburban bohemians, my parents actively fostered a song-filled house. Christmas brought new musical gifts: One year, it was two acoustic guitars in black cases with big red ribbons; another, it was a stereo; a third, Dad enlisted us kids' assistance in preparing a surprise for Mom. We covered a giant piece of brown paper with grade-school graffiti, then draped the improvised wrapping over a standup piano next to the Christmas tree. Mom feigned disbelief when she pulled off the homemade wrapping, but I can't imagine what else she thought it hid.

She never did learn to play, but Brett and I did. Always good students (perhaps because our parents were teachers), we learned how to sit properly at piano recitals, hold our hands just right, and make it through a piece of music without hitting too many wrong keys. We also tried our hands at guitar and viola. When I was around seven, I begged Mom and Dad to get me a drum kit like the one our neighbor Jon had, but that's where they drew the line. (Instead, I wound up spending years dating, living with, marrying, and raising drummers.) I think Brett and I both, separately, reluctantly, and inevitably, came to the conclusion that our rock-star ambitions would have to find other channels. Dreams, ideas, and love for music we had in spades, but the fact was, we lacked talent.

Mom had it though: She used to sing show tunes as she washed dishes or vacuumed the house, or just when she was happy. I loved to sing too but never had Mom's pipes, so I learned to keep my self-serenades discreet. Mostly, I sang out the car window. We spent our summer vacations pulling a trailer across America— probably the best education I ever got. I'd sit in the back seat on those long drives and toss my songs into the prairies, mountains, suburbs, and deserts.

Our trailer was our stagecoach and traveling classroom. We were pioneers, far from our roots, tight-knit, often tight-lipped. It was the era when the big-city AM stations carried music miles into the hinterlands and played the hits, and the hits were good. There were no cassettes, CDs, or satellite radio yet, and certainly no iPods into which we each plugged in separately. There was just the car radio, binding us all together with deliciously sugary pop and irresistible, saccharine ballads.

Brett was my best friend, sounding board, and think tank— when I could pull him out of his books. I remember having to coax him to play stuffed animals in the back seat; then he would only join if I let him be the rock star. He'd pick one plush toy to animate, while I'd man a cast of ten. Blacky, his Scotty (earned by sending in proofs of purchase from Scott tissue papers), was an Elvis in his depressive stage. While my tigers, koalas, cougars, and monkeys were arguing over recording contracts and tour plans, Blacky would be howling the saddest hound-dog song you ever heard. Once, he threw down his mike, stormed out of the studio, and disappeared into the night, shouting, "I don't want your money! No one understands me!"

I looked up at my red-faced brother with his hair in his eyes. *Okay.*

Brett and I shared 45s and LPs. He was at least as obsessed with music as I was, and since he was older, I learned about bands from him. He checked records out of the library: Joni Mitchell, Led Zeppelin, Cream. The first one bored me, and the second one scared me, but *Wheels of Fire*, I dug. When our ages were still in the single digits, I owned more 45s than he, but once we hit the doubles, his LP collection outpaced mine. I wasn't focused enough; I was buying clothes, jewelry, posters. Brett saved his allowance and lawn-mowing money every week, went to the local record store/head shop, and bought the latest releases he'd read about in *Rolling Stone* or the *Milwaukee Journal*: Elvis Costello, the Jam, Robert Johnson.

We were an intellectual family: well read, highly opinionated, and overly fond of puns. Mom and Dad discussed almost everything with us—politics, movies, music, current events, books, economics, psychology, sociology, history. We toured national parks and monuments, watched spewing geysers and Civil War reenactments. I vividly remember my parents' grimness when we visited Madison shortly after campus bombings there. They wanted Brett and me to see the dangers of extremism, how ideologues could tear apart the country, even in such a smart, lovely town as Madison. Like the times, Mom and Dad were leaving conservative shadows behind them. Democrats, Deweyians, Unitarians, they were also ahead of their time.

I remember once an older couple pulled alongside our brown Chevy station wagon, with our canoe on top, dog inside, and trailer behind. The woman rolled down her window and shouted, "You're so beautiful! The American dream!" Mom laughed so hard she started to cry.

Brett and I are demographic freaks: third-generation Californians, born in the same Glendale hospital as Dad and his dad. Our father was an only child whose beloved mother died when he was twelve; Gladys was the unknown heroine who haunted my childhood. Dad never forgave his father's quick remarriage. For birthdays and Christmas, the woman everyone called Sugar sent me perfume and jewelry, a collection that I kept shoved away in a drawer of my desk—femininity not discarded but banished.

Our left-coast legacy was cut short when we moved to Beloit, Wisconsin, when I was four. My brother and I were allergic to smog, Ronald Reagan was elected governor of California, and

Dad got a job as a professor at a small liberal arts college, so away we went.

My parents left their families thousands of miles away when we moved to Beloit. We didn't know anyone there, or in the state of Wisconsin, or really in the whole Midwest. We were like thousands of academic families, committed to the primacy of mind over matter, expected to plop down in a little American town and make it our own.

Our neighborhood was a place of solitude but not of fences, which meant we kids could run from the back of Scott's place, through three yards, past Joyrie's, to Jon's stone castle on the hill. Or we rode bikes. If you were really good—and lucky—you could start at the top of Jon's hill, lean sideways on the curve around Joyrie's, only have to pedal slightly up the gradual slope past Scott's, then glide down the ravine past my house and halfway up the other side—all with no hands. With a creek, field, and woods, Turtle Ridge was a bucolic setting for an active tomboy and a safe haven for her bookworm brother.

I was a child of the '70s. Women's liberation was not an ideal, but a fait accompli, as far as my skinny, barefoot self was concerned. Girls could do what the boys did, and no one cared. In fact, in our neighborhood, girly girls were uncool. Why be afraid to get your fingers dirty or a grass stain on your new pants? Wasn't that what jeans were for? I never wore a dress, a fact the snotty twins who moved in down the street noted with disdain—but then Jon, David, and Scott didn't play with Lisa and Jane, did they? I often didn't even wear a shirt, a taste for top freedom I got to revisit as an adult at gay-pride marches and then as a nursing mama. I loved being the girl who was one of the boys.

We'd left California, but California hadn't left us. In Beloit, we were strangers in a strange land: a little liberal, a little weird. Dad carried one of those male purses that were trendy in the '70s, which he bought in Amsterdam. The neighborhood kids laughed at that, but they loved our VW Bug, which we'd all pile into like some college fraternity prank on the days it was Dad's turn to drive the car pool to school.

Mama, Mom's mom, lived with us after Papa died, helping take care of Brett and me as best she could. My parents' discipline was too loose for her strict Baptist soul. I can remember her wanting to switch my backside on at least one occasion, probably because of my infamous ability to sass back. My parents, antispanking, wouldn't let her.

Mama was the family matriarch, but she was also an independent woman. She had once been a seamstress, making bathing suits in a factory, like the heroine of *Sister Carrie* or the victims of the Triangle Shirtwaist Fire. She eventually got tired of living in our basement and under our rules and moved into her own apartment. Every Wednesday when I was a teen, I would pick up Kentucky Fried Chicken and take it to Mama's place. She was always sewing, embroidering, or crocheting. She tried to teach me how to hold and work a needle, but I had no patience for such domestic endeavors. Sometimes she would try to convince me to adopt her Christian ways, shaking her head at my parents' agnosticism. Mostly, she was patient, kind, and accepting, devoted to her ever-expanding brood of children, grandchildren, and great-grandchildren.

Every few summers, we took our trailer out west, where we'd visit Mom's brothers. I loved my hard-working uncles with their pickup trucks and large families. Uncle John had a pool, which seemed like the best thing in the world. His kids, in their teens and twenties, were glamorous, beautiful, and tinged with tragedy, surviving car accidents and fiancées killed in plane crashes. With their beautiful, flowing manes and wide, easy California smiles, they all seemed like stars to me.

This was California's golden era. Cousin Cathy, two years older than me and so much cooler, literally taught me to speak its language. We listened to the Eagles, Fleetwood Mac, and Shaun Cassidy; we watched *Charlie's Angels, The Hardy Boys,* and *CHIPS*; we perused *Teen Beat* and *Tiger Beat.* My jaw would drop at her stories about celebrities she had seen in grocery stores, malls, or cars. She was, literally, a valley girl, a resident of San Fernando, and she taught me to say "like," "for sure," and "tubular," even before Frank and Moon Zappa had a hit making fun of teen dialect. (Years later, in the late '90s, punk feminist Kathleen Hanna reclaimed this mode of communication as part of grrrls' unique way of being, recording the song "V.G.I.," short for Valley Girl Intelligentsia, under the name Julie Ruin. Like, for sure, talking in tongues was a way Cathy and I connected and asserted our difference, our youth, our generation.)

Like young girls everywhere, we would sneak out at night to wander, mostly just talking. We had no destination; it was all about the journey and the transgression. Occasionally, terrifyingly, helicopters would fly low overhead, shining spotlights on the mostly deserted streets. I doubt they were looking for petty curfew breakers like us, but still we hid under cars. L.A. was like that, a place brimming with boredom and chaos, teetering between fascism and anarchy.

Wisconsin offered woodsiness and four-season adventures. But sometimes, when I felt like I didn't fit in, when I was a little wild for conservative Midwestern values, particularly as I got older and hormones started making me restless, California was a beautiful, seductive, glamorous siren. I believed its was the lifestyle to which I had, literally, been born: backyard pools, movie stars on the corner, sea and sun, and the wind in my hair.

Michael Jackson was the knight of my California dreaming; then, it was Shaun Cassidy; then, the Beatles. And then, it was Bruce Springsteen, who sang about workers like my uncles, about the factories closing around us in Beloit, about little girls driving alone through the Wisconsin night.

By the time I fell for the Boss, adolescence had changed everything. Girls and boys didn't play the same way anymore; home was a place to get away from, not to. Then, Reagan was elected president. Where could we run to this time?

2

Queens of Noise

⊘ ⊘ ⊘

I remember the precise moment my blue-jeaned belief that the sexes had achieved social equality came crashing down around me: I was biking to the first day of junior high with Scott, Jon, and David, my neighborhood crew of boys. From banana seats and ape-hanger handlebars, we had graduated to bikes with clinking gearshifts and spring-loaded hand brakes, over whose curved handlebars we bent low for maximum speed. Pedaling the mile plus, the boys kept racing ahead. I kept catching up. Silently, they would go faster.

"Guys, wait up! What's the hurry?"

No answer, feet pumping.

"What's happening? Did I do something wrong?"

Silence. Faster. Catch up.

Finally, Scott, the freckle-faced blond who lived across the street, the quickest kid on the block despite his short stature, the friend who in my secret heart was my best friend, my soul mate, my Tom Sawyer, kicked a foot out at my olive-green Raleigh, sending me veering across the blacktop and almost into some stranger's lawn.

"You're a girl!" Scott shouted, laying the new rules on the line. "Go away!"

Adolescence is the miserable age of innocence lost, yet maturity far from gained. I entered it as ungracefully as possible: unbecoming, short pixie haircut, big plastic glasses, geek-defining acne, and a taste for colorful, dated hippie garb. I didn't help matters by proclaiming to my English class that I believed in magic. I would stroll into the parking lot at lunchtime, and kids would actually point and laugh.

Culture was in a period of awkward transition too. The Vietnam War was over, a Democrat was (briefly) in the White House, and the rock era was about to end. In urban ghettos, new sounds—disco, reggae, hip-hop, punk—were shaking up the 4/4 beat. But they were only slowly slipping their dissonance into a Midwest still savoring the false utopia of "Rock 'n' roll Hoochie Koo," as Rick Derringer so eloquently put it.

Two women sprung me from Hoochie Koo hell. The first was blonde, solid, and by my side almost daily; the second was dark, disheveled, and a far-off icon. At a time when I was supposed to be thinking of nothing but boys, boys, boys, they taught me the priceless value of the female. The light one anchored me. "Transcend, transcend," the dark one chanted.

Cindy had everything I didn't: blond hair, statuesque boobs. As she said in a speech at my first wedding decades later, "I was a cheerleader. Evelyn was not." She didn't just wave pom-poms at athletes; she was one too, taking full advantage of Title IX's level playing field to excel at softball, volleyball, tennis, basketball. I, despite my tree-climbing youth, was retreating into true nerd mode and slouching against the wall during gym class. I had run into the wall of hormones that knocks tomboys off their barefooting, and I was still wobbling.

Cindy just shrugged her linebacker shoulders. With her Scandinavian coloring, easy demeanor, and developed bosom, she made butch beautiful. She could feather her hair just right and hit a home run, making both the boys and the girls feel comfortable around her. She was the rosy-cheeked apotheosis of '70s Midwestern values: kind, direct, industrious. I honestly don't think there was anyone at our school who didn't like her. She was also a math prodigy whose dad worked the assembly line at the General Motors plant and whose mom stayed home and raised three kids—working-class heroes are something to be. And for some blessed reason, she was the best friend of freaky, geeky me.

We would spend practically the whole day together, then talk on the phone every night, rehashing events, stamping them with our own interpretations and approving each other's stamps.

"Kirk asked me to go with him," Cindy would say. Kirk was a grade above us, a tall, thin boy with a head of scalp-hugging curls.

"What'd you tell him?" I'd ask. No one ever asked me to go with them.

"Yes, of course! He's cute."

"He's cute. I asked Paul to go to a movie with me."

"Good for you! What did he say?"

"He said yes. But it was a pity yes. And then everyone started making fun of him."

"They did not!"

"Did too!"

"Oh, I've got to go. My half-hour's up." Cindy's strict dad put time limits on how long she could talk on the phone.

With Cindy's help, I learned to blow-dry my hair and get a cowl neck to lie just right, so its folds could be pierced by a stickpin. I exchanged the four-eyes frames for contact lenses, grew my hair long enough to approximate the Farrah Fawcett look, and left the dashikis in the closet. By the time we started high school, I had landed that most valuable of assets: a popular, older boyfriend.

Vince was a drummer, the first in a long line of percussionists who have punctuated my opera with their cymbal crashes, snares, and drumrolls. He was a big-nosed, curly-haired boy, a bit of a roughneck Italian. One time, he cut his hand after smashing it through a window. He had a sweet side too. When I lost my cat, he gave me a little orange kitten, whom I dubbed Vinnie, for my birthday.

We didn't have a lot in common, except for love of rock 'n' roll. My tomboyism had morphed into a fixation with guitar bands. I might have struggled with the art of the curling iron, but I could hold my own with a group of guys dissecting Jimmy Page solos, no problem. Vince's band became my new neighborhood gang. My drummer boy even wrote a song about me; "Natural High" was sweet and corny. I hung out at rehearsals, went to their shows at parks and malls. There was something sexy about guys with instruments, even in the middle of a shopping plaza. Vince and I would make out in his basement to Cheap Trick records. Cheap Trick was from nearby Rockford, Illinois, so they were hometown heroes. We did a lot of dry humping, but there was no genital contact: "Surrender, surrender, but don't give yourself away," Robin Zander would sing.

Vince and Cindy gave me ninth-grade cultural cachet. Whereas the popular girls and the stoners had once closed ranks against me, I could now sit with the cheerleaders at lunch or smoke a joint in the empty field across from the school.

The only problem: I was bored.

Cousin Cathy, connoisseur of all things cool, first told me about a strange music and fashion coming from New York and London. Hers was not a recommendation. "Punks actually like things and people that are ugly," she told me. "Like, they think ugly is cool. Grody."

At first, I of course agreed with Cathy: punk = grody. But, gradually, it occurred to me that people in New York and London thought ugly was cool; meanwhile, I was spending hours of my day struggling to control acne outbreaks and keep curls in line, to make myself look "pretty" for people who, in truth, were rather dull. If I just let myself be ugly, punks would think I was cool! By tenth grade, I had traded stickpins for safety pins.

Surrounded by cows and cowl-necks, I was a small-town middle-American wannabe trying to connect with a scene thousands of miles away and a couple years past. Yet when I heard the Ramones singing "Sheena Is a Punk Rocker" or the Jam describing "Saturday's Kids," I heard my life. Wherever we were, we were all suffering under the same millennial mania for a "Germ-free Adolescence," as X-Ray Spex lamented. We were looking for a culture that was ours, not the emerging sellout of the baby boomers.

Beloit was not exactly a hot spot for new wave fashion. My first sartorial statement fulfilled punk's do-it-yourself ethos: I ripped a white T-shirt, connected the holes with safety pins, and wrote the names of my new favorite bands in Magic Marker: Sex Pistols, the Ramones, the Clash. The local Salvation Army yielded treasures, including two black-and-white miniskirt outfits—so ska. And then there was Madison; an hour's drive away, the state capital and university town was Mecca for my small group of new wave misfits. It's where we went for books, records, clothes, pot pipes, and *The Rocky Horror Picture Show*. We found cool Devo wraparound shades and little new wave buttons galore, declaring, "Fuck art, let's dance," "Blondie is a band," and "Fuck authority." Woody Guthrie was wrong: We needed badges.

We were imitating the few stories we saw in magazines and the covers of our favorite records. It wasn't like we could sneak over to shows at CBGB's and suss out the latest style, like my future friends from New York did. There *was* Summerfest. It was in these familiar, familial stomping grounds that I saw my first new wave concert. While my parents were watching Brubeck, I was up front at Squeeze, pogoing my heart out. The power-pop band wasn't punk rock, but they were English, bouncy, and had short hair. A guy with a full rockabilly pompadour, peg-leg pants, and striped blazer with skinny lapels bobbed next to me. He looked me in the face, gave me a big kiss on the lips, then pogoed off. Yes, I had found my people.

Smearing KY jelly into my shorn locks to make them stand up spikey didn't exactly make me popular. Vince broke up with me; I never had another high school boyfriend. But who cared, when I had the Clash? Their music was taut with a tension and passion as acute as my teenage being. Plus, they were political. And they were so fucking cute. Bassist Paul Simonon: Jesus Christ, could a man get any sexier? The Clash let their fans crash in their hotel rooms, I read in *Rolling Stone*, not as some kind of orgy but as a communal vibe. That seemed so much more real than the haughty distance and groupie groping of the long-haired, wannabe Dionysian rock gods.

And the women. I came of age in an era with powerful icons who didn't just look the part, but wrote songs, played instruments, and created fashion. The Pretenders' Chrissie Hynde was precious: She had brass in pocket, she snarled "fuck off," and moved from Ohio to London with a Stooges album as cultural passport. Debbie Harry was dead sexy and cool, her tongue lodged firmly in her impossibly high cheekbone. Like the Runaways before them, the Go-Go's took the posse spirit of the rock band and made it a safe place to have endless summer beach-girls fun. Tina Weymouth was the tomboy bassist, holding her own with the boys of Talking Heads.

Mostly, there was Patti Smith.

I must have first seen her on *Saturday Night Live*, where she performed like a banshee shaman. In her ragged poet's garb, she seemed both otherworldly and raw, to have me locked in her trance and to be fiercely present. I had never seen any woman quite like that—so thoroughly unobjectified, so hairy, sexy, skinny, and strong. Soon, I was entranced with her *Easter* album. Its haunted spirituality spoke to my troubled, agnostic soul. "Have I doubt, when I'm alone/Love is a ring, the telephone/Love is an angel, disguised as lust/Here in our bed until the morning comes." Smith sang how a lonely teenage girl felt, wanting to be loved and fucked. Her voice was so different from any other women's I had heard—deep and hoarse, the gravel-road opposite of Mom's soaring trills. With guitars exploding and keyboards crashing, her songs about ghostly siblings and space monkeys were as intense as a once carefree little girl exploding with adolescent hormone rush, with rage at new social confinements and desire to be anywhere but where she was, anywhere in the "sea of possibilities," as Patti sang.

A poster of the album cover hung on my bedroom wall. In the photo by her best friend, Robert Mapplethorpe, Smith wears a peach camisole. Her arm is raised and her pit unshaven. You can see her braless breasts through the delicate cloth. Patti's dark tangled hair is long but not feathered. She looks radically feminine and radiantly beautiful.

I've met scores of women and men for whom Smith, in her trousers and tie, redefined their notion of how one could be and look sexually. She made lesbians and bisexuals feel safe because in "Gloria" and "Redondo Beach," she sang love songs for women. To this day, I don't shave my underarms and rarely wear a bra, in part because of that *Easter* poster. Patti was a tomboy woman who had carved out her own bike path, one boys raced down to follow.

Patti was a writer, and so was I. She began her career as a poet and sometime rock critic. That seemed like an interesting job, I thought: rock critic.

Vince left, but Cindy was steadfast. We did homework together, edited the newspaper, had secondary roles in the school plays, worked at a drive-in movie theater, ripped the tops off of cornstalks. We talked about college, which we both knew we were going to attend. We talked about boys, often. But I don't remember us ever talking about having kids.

Cindy's mom, Janet, and I drove her to college in the late summer of '82. Admiring her brains, athleticism, and tremendous friendship, my parents had helped steer Cindy to a nice scholarship at a tony private college outside Chicago. Janet and I dropped this prole babe with her public school diploma into a world marred by boarding school brats whose grades hadn't been good enough to get them in an Eastern school, no matter how much money daddy pledged to the endowment. In a week, I'd be shipping out myself, to the Ivy League, lord help me.

On the way home, Cindy's mom spoke to me as an adult.

"I hate to see my last one go," she said. I heard a pinch in her tired, flat, Midwestern drawl.

"She'll be okay. Cindy can handle herself."

"I know she will be. I know she can. She's getting a chance to see the world. That's what I want for her: to have more than I did, not to just get married and have kids."

"But you have great kids."

"Yes. But a woman needs more."

There was a resolve in Janet's tone, a subtle fighting streak I had always known was there, though she let her husband set the house rules. Years later, after Cindy graduated and her father retired, Janet left Roy for a while, took her own apartment, went back to school, and started working. Late in life, she began doing the things she had missed out on, which she seemed to see shimmering before her on the highway like blacktop mirages on that late-summer drive. That's what our mothers wanted us to enjoy: all those opportunities nixed by piles of dishes to clean. Out of women's liberation came girls' liberation. We were lucky to be its pioneers.

3

Set It Off

∞ ∞ ∞

It was a Thursday night at Rocket and I was playing DJ. I was also running behind the bar to help mix Rocket's signature blue drinks and darting backstage to make sure the headlining band was doing okay. I had hired them, after all, just as I booked all of the out-of-town bands that played here. Like most of the acts that passed through this downtown Providence new wave joint, these guys—actually, two men and a woman drummer—were from New Jersey. They were stopping here to pick up some extra cash between bigger gigs in New Haven and Boston. It was 1987, and there was a growing network of small labels, clubs, fanzines, and college radio stations supporting musicians who had something besides the Top 40 on their minds.

I was on a song roll, completing a trifecta of moody, primitive-sounding, art brut rock 'n' roll: "Why Don't You Smile Now," a track recorded in the '60s by Lou Reed before he was in the Velvet Underground; "Her Parents Came Home," a Half Japanese tune in which Jad Fair warbles with fractured sensitivity; and "You're No Good" by the funky postpunk girl group ESG. It wasn't what you would call a dance set, but beneath the raw production and feedback noise were desultory beats and desired melodies.

The New Jersey guitarist walked over. I knew Ira was a some-time journalist and connoisseur of arcane musicana. I knew be-cause, before they came to town, I had interviewed him for an article for the local alternative newspaper. He personified the quiet intellect and sometimes self-righteousness of collegiate col-lectors, a somber demeanor that I, too, was trying to affect (when I wasn't plastered on blue drinks).

"Hi," I said, coming down from the DJ booth. "Can I get you something?"

"We're cool. I just wanted to know, did you get that first song off that new Velvets box set?"

"Yeah." In addition to booking Rocket and writing for *The New Paper,* I clerked at a local record store, where a discount allowed me to afford box sets.

"You're playing some really great records," he said, surprisingly sweetly. I knew Ira was a Velvets fan; you just had to listen to his band's music to figure that out. "Very impressive. Thanks."

"Thank you!"

Then Ira Kaplan went off to lead Yo La Tengo through a relent-lessly smart set of guitar pop (even though there were only about fifty people in Rocket) and the burgeoning indie-rock scene to a state of instrumental erudition.

I went away to college and wound up in the clubs.

My time at college was supposed to be my wonder years, or so my parents had led me to believe. After all, in college they had both escaped their families and met each other. And I had scored:

I got into Brown, the "it" school of the '80s. I rubbed shoulders with political scions and movie stars, with John Kennedy Jr., the prince of Jordan, and Amy Carter. Even Ringo Starr sent his daughter to Brown.

Mostly, I was miserable. Brown was stuffy, and Brown was hard. I was outclassed in more ways than one. In high school, hard work made me class valedictorian, and punk rock made me an iconoclast. At the Berkeley of the Ivy League, I was a rube among sophisticates, a Midwestern, public school graduate surrounded by preppies and Eurotrash. Records that had been rare in Beloit were standard fare for sophisticated kids from New York, London, and Los Angeles; in fact, they were probably passé. Far from being edgy, I was looked at as a denizen of "the flyover," the great, unwashed middle of the country that my classmates only saw from airplane windows en route between the coasts. It amazed me that these prep school graduates couldn't find Wisconsin on a map, but they could breeze through Julia Kristeva, while I hacked my way through the jargon jungle. I struggled to figure out what the hell semiotics was—did it have something to do with idiotics, or was it just me?

Most excruciatingly embarrassing were my eating habits, products both of being raised in landlocked suburbia by a working mother and, I'll admit it, of being a bit of a picky princess: a glass of Pillsbury Instant Breakfast in the morning, Mountain Dew as a caffeine source (I hated coffee), SpaghettiOs and Little Debbies for snacks. The only dinners I could cook were made in casserole dishes, including one of my favorites: canned tuna mixed with cream of mushroom soup and topped with crushed potato chips.

This, while the cool urbanites I looked up to at Brown nibbled sushi, were connoisseurs of couscous, could detail the differences between Thai, Vietnamese, and Mandarin cuisine (wasn't it all stir-fry?). They didn't call those Italian noodles topped with tomato sauce spaghetti; they called them pasta.

I quickly found refuge in noise.

Freshman year found me sharing a room smaller than my Beloit bedroom with a drummer from Florida who also worshipped the Clash. In a way Vince never did, Regina taught me to listen to music as a musician, to hear how the instruments worked — or didn't work — together. I hung out at her band's practices, became a fourth wheel for the quirky pop trio. Regina was tall and wore big skirts; I was short and lived in a pair of old black ski pants. We both had angular new wave hairdos. And despite being considerably better off financially than I, she was equally unhappy at Brown.

We were hard-nosed in our musical and lifestyle choices. For instance, we decided David Bowie had sold out with the lame disco anthem "Let's Dance." We blamed the erstwhile gay icon's softness on his having fallen in love with a woman, on having become so conventional, so '80s. Regina was interested in drumming, and I was interested in taking in as much live music as I possibly could. This was the foundation of our friendship.

One night, while our fellow dormmates were heading to a mixer, we trudged to an Iggy Pop concert off campus. We got to the rundown hall early and staked out positions in the front row. Iggy was the dark muse behind Bowie's happy dance act (it was rumored that the Brit and the Motor City madman had been lovers). And while Mr. Pop did not lacerate himself on stage that night, as he was known to do, he was still the most intense, disturbed, and disturbing performer I had yet seen, maybe ever have seen. The band's music was thick, depressive, exhilarating. At one point, Iggy, his skinny, bare chest and rope arms drenched with sweat, fixed us with his giant, dark eyes and moaned as if he could pour psychosis out of his gaping orbs into ours. Regina was sure it was her he sang to, that he recognized and connected with a fellow perturbed musician soul. She had some deep understanding of the music that night that gave her a smug serenity for days and weeks afterward. I thought Iggy saw me too.

Trying so hard to be hard, I could be my own worst enemy. I was resolutely unsentimental. I hated slow songs, love songs, bathetic ballads. (Though there were a few rhapsodies in blue — Marvin Gaye's "Sexual Healing," John Lennon's "You've Got to Hide Your Love Away," Joy Division's "Love Will Tear Us Apart" — that could make me secretly break down in tears.) I loved to pogo but refused to slow dance. I liked rap but couldn't stomach the Quiet Storm format, with all that Luther Vandross overemoting.

You weren't likely to find Regina and me at the Sarah Doyle Women's Center or any other feminist campus gathering. Still, we knew we were pioneer girls invading boy terrain. We were determined not to fall into the standard female rocker modes: earth mother, groupie, or dyke. We bedded musicians but had no interest in wedding them. My attitude toward children was summarized by my fondness for dead baby jokes. I adopted a scene from the Andy Warhol movie *Bad* as a symbol of my revolt against the idea that maternity equals womanhood: A Jackie O–looking character is standing in her high-rise apartment, bored, agitated, smoking a cigarette. Her crying baby finally pushes her over the edge, and she very nonchalantly drops the infant out the window to the pavement below, where it splatters on a screaming young woman.

By the end of that first year of college, I had mastered my escape routes to Providence's several decent clubs. Sometimes, I would walk miles through downtown streets by myself, guitars still ringing in my ears from a concert as I neared the campus. Rashly, perhaps, I was never scared; it was I, stomping in my combat boots, who had a habit of coming up on canoodling college couples on leafy streets and startling them apart.

There was only one musical event that was cool enough for school, that kept me on campus every Thursday: Funk Night.

At Funk Night, DJs with direct channels to New York spun the latest sounds from club land: Prince, Michael Jackson, Slick Rick, the Gap Band, George Clinton, the real Roxanne. It was here, in the Brown pub, that I got my first hint that there could be such a thing as a hip-hop generation, though it wasn't quite our generation: We still had the funk, the electro, a little new wave. In Beloit, I had heard rap mostly through the new wave groups: Blondie's "Rapture," the Tom Tom Club's "Genius of Love" and "Wordy Rappinghood," the Clash's "The Magnificent Seven." Then, Grandmaster Flash and the Furious Five's "The Message" had been a freshman-year anthem. It was clearly a song about ghetto life, but when Melle Mel rapped about being close to the edge, this white Midwesterner could relate.

Funk Night was where I also realized the power of the club jockey; in the '80s and '90s, a DJ was as likely as a band to save one's life. My favorite songs had raw, slinky pulses: Spoonie Gee's

"The Big Beat," a primitive single from Philadelphia with the sound of a mattress squeaking for not-so-subtle percussive effect, and Strafe's "Set It Off," a whispered call to get the party started right. Both were short on lyrical content but brilliant in their beats—protocrunk, if you will.

The Raiford sisters, Wanda and Janice, were my Funk Night dance partners. We met while cleaning dorms one summer. Wanda and I discovered that we were both pot fiends with similarly obsessive, cavalier attitudes about guys and sex. We wound up living off campus together our senior year, the first time I ever began to feel at home away from Beloit.

Wanda and I were like husband and wife. I was the one who worked outside the home, going to clubs, writing for the local weekly newspaper. She liked to hang around the apartment, watch TV in her bra, do her nails. We stocked our kitchen with plates and flatware stolen from our catering jobs. It was a typically bare-bones, run-down student flat. Our gangly landlord seemed rather mafioso, not a stretch of the imagination in Italian-thick Providence. Toward year's end, the bathroom ceiling collapsed, and we had to hold an umbrella while sitting on the toilet. There was a big, orange neighborhood cat we fed and let sleep on our couch.

Wanda was probably the sagest person I knew. I could tell her a little problem, and she would immediately get the big picture and put it all into humorous perspective. When a friend confessed to us that she had never had an orgasm, Wanda and I got to work to address this serious problem. We taught Veronica all we knew about vibrators and the importance of oral sex. We also recommended she stop dating frat boys.

Wanda got me. All bad-ass and music-obsessed, I was probably the least maternal woman around. Settling down and getting married was as far from my twenty-one-year-old mind as buying a suit for job interviews, which is what my intelligent classmates, like Wanda, were doing. Yet years later, when, by the weird twists of fate, I became the one finally to have a baby, Wanda said, "You always had a good mama inside you. That's why you took care of that cat." I didn't know anyone saw me that way, but, of course, Cole proved Wanda right.

I formed a lasting bond with one other Brown classmate, and music was part of our glue too. Brian was sweet, smart, and savagely funny. I met him one summer at Brown's special collections library, where we both worked, pulling H. P. Lovecraft's musty manuscripts out of the basement. A Michigander with shoulder-length, golden-blond hair, a funny nose, and pale blue eyes, Brian had a brown scar on his skinny torso from when he was born and nearly died. His mother died of cancer a couple years before we met. There was an undercurrent of morbid melancholy in Brian, which might have brought out that mother Wanda saw in me. Brian was my first real boyfriend who wasn't a bit of a schmuck or a bundle of trouble. I had a thing for bad guys, tough cases, rebels without causes. Brian was a tragic figure, a sarcastic fuck, who looked a little like Jesus Christ and Pete Townsend. But he was a good guy—a brilliant guy. The day I read a script he had written sealed the deal. Like all of his plays, it was a tragicomedy that took an absurdist set piece—in this case, a nativity scene—and therein excavated humanity in all its beloved peculiarities. In the '90s and aughties, a trilogy called *Americana Absurdum* took

Brian Parks to Edinburgh and London, making him the world-famous scribe I always thought he should be.

Brian and I bonded as Midwesterners displaced to one of the oldest states in the union. Periodically, on special occasions or not, he would buy me a dozen gorgeous pastel roses, even years after we broke up. He wasn't tough, or strong, or wild. So, of course, I eventually got bored. I was a no-good, heartbreak woman, unable or unwilling to roost in one bed for long. But my friendship with Brian has survived everything: moves, marriages, breakdowns, our mutual employment by the *Village Voice*, terrorist attacks, the breakup of Camper Van Beethoven.

Brian was like my brother Brett: a couple years older, bookish, fragile, gentle, and into music. He turned me on to bands: the Feelies, the Mekons, the Replacements, American Music Club. He wasn't a hipster, trying to show off and be indier than thou with his gourmet taste in nouveau sounds. He just liked albums the way some people like books. Besides, college/alternative/indie rock wasn't quite an entity yet, a school to which one swore allegiance; it was being born before our ears.

Music was bifurcating. The airwaves and arenas were dominated by superbig commercial entities: Springsteen, Madonna, Michael Jackson, U2. Those mega-acts seemed distant, unreal; their music sounded synthetic, produced. Even my beloved Bruce had gone mainstream with the fist-thumping, flag-waving, if ironically misunderstood, "Born in the U.S.A."

Conservative radio playlists helped keep punk from conquering the United States the way it had taken over England, but the music infiltrated. Via such regional labels as TwinTone and SST, bands like the Meat Puppets, Hüsker Dü, and Sonic Youth were making intricate, intimate rock 'n' roll. You could go see these bands, up front and personal, in small clubs. Some of the music was political; the Minutemen tore the guts out of Woody Guthrie's "Badges." Some was drunken and cathartic; "Outside this bar, there's no one alive," American Music Club's Mark Eitzel wailed for the lonely hearts. Some was just extraordinarily well played; how did the Feelies make strummed guitar music so fast and precise?

And all of these bands and more came to town. Situated between Boston and New York, Providence was a regular stop for bands touring the Northeast. The same acts that would play in front of packed, large venues elsewhere might perform in front of one hundred people at the Living Room, Lupo's Heartbreak Hotel, the Last Call Saloon, or the Rocket. The Mekons, R.E.M., Live Skull, Big Black, Butthole Surfers, the Cramps, Nina Hagen, Green on Red, Divine Horsemen, Young Fresh Fellows, Gutbank, Billy Bragg, Run DMC, the Church: Every week, it was a different act. The Pixies, Christmas, and Big Dipper were locals from Boston; they were guys and girls we'd see around. I was spending as much time listening to records as reading books. That was okay; by the time I graduated, I had decided to pursue a career in music.

I collected my first rock-crit paycheck senior year. I'd sent a bunch of articles I'd written for campus publications to *The New-Paper*, Rhode Island's free weekly. Editor Lou Papineau kindly asked me to interview a Newport band that was getting a lot of buzz: the female-fronted Throwing Muses. Talking with the band, I was impressed with their sisterly nerve and Velvet Underground appreciation. The article concluded, "Kristin Hersh and

Tanya Donnelly aren't anyone's blondes." I was thrilled a week later to collect my $50.

The NewPaper turned into steady work. It didn't pay much, but it was better than trying to find an unpaid internship in New York or writing obits for some small-town newspaper. To help pay the bills, I got the Rocket and record-store gigs. With a group of friends—musicians, artists, and writers—I published a fanzine, OK Go Now. Regina, the drummer, and I became roommates again. Our wood-floored apartment was a sometime flophouse for bands that couldn't afford hotels.

Wearing so many hats caused ethical conflicts, like writing about acts I had booked. But if no one else had the good sense to interview the Flaming Lips in 1987, what else was a girl to do? Despite my best efforts, only a couple dozen people came to see Wayne Coyne resurrect psychedelia at the Rocket. We were building a new scene in a small city not known for its hipness. Sometimes, I felt like Sisyphus.

Rhode Island is a strange state. It's small, obviously. And yet, I was amazed by how many people I met there rarely, if ever, left its borders. In some ways, Providence felt even more provincial than Beloit. New England can be a cold place, physically and emotionally. I hated walking down Boston's streets, all those white faces hunched into bulky sweaters, not looking at each other. Brrrr.

After six years there, I started to feel as if Providence—like Beloit, like Brown—was trying to fit me into its preconceived notions, its finite atmosphere. I was holding out for the infinite.

4

New York Woman

Oo   Oo   Oo

In 1991 an artist named Rodrigo Pascal filled the walls of the
Nuyorican Poets Café with brightly colored portraits of denizens
of that downtown performance space. Drawn with paint crayons
on typing-paper-sized pieces of particle board, the paintings
weren't brilliant in their detail or finesse. Rodrigo, a tender-eyed
Puerto Rican, dashed them out in quick sittings sped by buoyant
talk. He drew heads only, capturing expressions, shapes, and light
in splashes of primary and flesh colors—flesh in all its shades,
from charcoal to clay to sand.

This art wasn't about individual notes; it was about the symphony. Rodrigo painted a panorama in parts of the people that
transformed a time and place. Like the Nuyorican, like Loisaida,
like the early '90s, like artistic egos, like movements in the making, like poetry itself, the works were vibrantly of the moment—a
moment when all at once, in one room, masterpieces were created, careers born, romances forged, arms broken, and history
made.

Hundreds of faces stared back at themselves at the exhibit's opening night: poets, novelists, artists, musicians, actors, playwrights, journalists. High on one wall was the image of a white woman in her twenties with streaked light-brown hair. At least for the length of an art show, my wandering soul had found a cranny.

The trick in leaving home is to make a new home. In my dozen years in New York, I found several substitute families: a newspaper, a café, an activist group, a magazine, a musical, a circle of friends. Some were more functional than others; some lasted years, some a meteoric moment.

New York was an inevitable destination that I stubbornly resisted. Small-town America had infused me with Gothamphobia: A girl like me was sure to get raped and killed while hundreds ignored my dying screams. New York was too busy, stinky, polluted, expensive, crowded. "All those people living on top of each other," a guy in suburban Utah put it to me once, shaking his head at the outrageous idea of humanity en masse. "Ugh."

I swallowed the lines. I was known to rage against New York's immorality: people lying in gutters while swells dined warm and safe in their townhouses. I hated New Yorkers' arrogance, pretentiousness, and privilege. After I'd worked for New York magazines for a dozen years, my opinion changed little; I still believe the city's tastemakers and pundits can be woefully out of touch with the rest of the country. I just came to appreciate the fact that sometimes that's a good thing.

Lou Reed was the first male to lure me to the Big Apple with his siren song. Freshman year I road-tripped to see the bard of anomie play the Bottom Line, a small club nestled between New

York University buildings. Reed was up there with Smith and Springsteen in my pantheon of musician deities: He was Pluto, the dark god, connoisseur of decadence and depravity, of transvestites, junkies, sadomasochists, and Andy Warhol. And yet, he was a guy who still believed a life could be saved by rock 'n' roll.

Before the concert, Brett met my friends and me in the city. We spent the day shopping, eating, walking, and drinking. Unique Boutique, Canal Jeans, Trash and Vaudeville: I was a small-town babe soaking up downtown's mercantile marvels—and being shocked as I stepped over homeless people asleep on the sidewalk in a city obviously stuffed with wealth. It was Reagan's America, a throwback to Depression days. By the time the rock 'n' roll animal finally came on at midnight, I was so exhausted I could barely keep my eyes open.

After that, I made semiyearly pilgrimages to Patti and Bruce's former stomping ground. Brian took me there for a weekend of theater, food, and sightseeing. Regina and I visited increasingly often, usually driving the VW Rabbit her parents had given her. Our hearts would soar when we'd get onto the George Washington Bridge and see Manhattan before us like a concrete Candyland. Sometimes, stoned, we'd get lost on East Village streets, where we circled repeatedly, desperately searching for parking. Somehow, we always wound up in front of a five-story tenement we dubbed Big Pink because of the paint job that made it stand out like a giant Day-Glo flower. Then, we'd know where we were: midway between CBGB's and St. Mark's Place. We'd eat steamed vegetables with melted cheese—a cheap, healthy stomach filler—at Dojo's, the Japanese diner. Once, our Boston friends Big Dipper opened for the Pogues at Irving Plaza. Drunken singer Shane

MacGowan had managed to get himself booted from the Irish outfit, but he'd been replaced by the Clash's Joe Strummer, so the change was more than okay. When Regina and I walked by the rooster-haired Strummer on the street outside the venue, we elbowed each other surreptitiously. After he passed, we melted into giggles, like two schoolgirls who'd just walked by the cutest upperclassman.

I began to visit New York for music-industry events: the one-stop-shopping gigstravaganza of the late, great New Music Seminar and the conference sponsored by the *College Media Journal* (CMJ). One Halloween, I was the token female on a critics panel at CMJ (an experience that got me immortalized as "Ursulina" in a *Spin* cartoon). That night, I fell in with a group of writers and musicians, including the king and queen of überhipsters, Kim Gordon and Thurston Moore of Sonic Youth. We wandered the Village, which was full of more tricks than treats. The streets had descended into near anarchy, or so it seemed to awestruck me. The cops had blocked off whole trash-strewn blocks. We were supposed to be checking out clubs packed with bands, but the night outside was too spellbinding. Walls were collapsing in Eastern Europe. Something was in the air.

Love brought me to New York. Or at least that was my excuse.

Jeff and I met in Providence. He was a graduate of the Rhode Island School of Design, the art school that abutted Brown physically but ran perpendicular culturally. An illustrator, animator, and graphic designer, Jeff played guitar in a band with Regina. Dirt Road's music provided a low-fi tour of dusty American byways—blues and country and punk held together with piss and snot. Other members went on to bands that were famous-only-in-New-York-and-among-a-handful-of-snarky-fanzine-readers: Cop Shoot Cop, Railroad Jerk, and Cobalt. This galaxy of artists and musicians, with former Brown student Jon Spencer of Pussy Galore infamy as its black hole sun, was a tiny, big-headed scene. Its surly guys and ultracool chicks hid their diplomas and pedigrees behind carefully careless grooming and heroin addictions. Maybe they had fucked-up family situations; still, they thought compassion was for pussies.

Whereas the punk I teethed on was idealistic and even earnest (therefore, easily mocked), these postpunks were nihilists. Postmodernism had replaced modernism: Writers of literary criticism, but not of literature, had declared truth criminal (an act of chutzpah that would be roughly equivalent to my music-crit colleagues' declaring harmony dead). Spencer—who made at least one brilliant film at Brown, a visit inside a slaughterhouse that left the audience at a student film festival mute—eviscerated politically correct sensibilities with songs called "You Look Like a Jew" and "Cunt Tease." By the time I arrived in New York, the city's hipsters were in his dark, handsome thrall.

Ohio-bred Jeff was too sweet for this edifice of attitude. Sure enough, shortly after I moved to the city to join him in his Queens flat, his songwriting partner dumped him. Like Paul McCartney turning to Linda (though as a budding rock critic, I was probably more loathed among Jeff's peers than a Yoko Ono), Jeff began teaching me riffs on the electric blue Washburn I'd bought. We'd sit on the wooden floor of our narrow Long Island City apartment, in front of his boa constrictor coiled in its tank, practicing "I Wanna Be Your Dog," "Clash City Rockers," or songs Jeff wrote.

He was the first guy I lived with, guinea pig darling. His lash-framed brown eyes had a flash point: He'd be looking at you, and suddenly something would click—there would be this whole other level of light. That look, that spark, indicated intrigue, unexplored depth, a secret cavern to go spelunking down. I tied a rope around my waist and plunged.

Jeff designed my first tattoo: The tribal black cat with a swirling body is a tribute to Brendalyn, my longtime feline companion. A bearded man with the dubious moniker Rusty sank his needles into my lower back in a small alley shop in Providence's Italian district. Tattoos were just beginning to be hip. They were emblems of the modern primitives movement, the gateway scarification ritual for an emergent subculture in which people showed their disaffection for civilization by piercing, branding, and torturing themselves. Hippies had marches and be-ins; we had fetish parties and deformance art.

In the 1980s, *Billboard* was headquartered in a skyscraper in the heart of Times Square. (The magazine has since moved, and now 1515 Broadway is the building MTV has made famous with live broadcasts from its second floor studio.) I landed a part-time job there, copyediting the dominant trade publication of the music industry, checking writers' p's and q's and penning headlines. My plan was to parlay that inside track and some other connections into writing assignments. Two or three days a week, I took the train to *Billboard*'s offices near 42nd and Broadway. Times Square hadn't been "cleaned up" yet, though I didn't mind its mix of cheese and squalor. Sure, peep shows offered alternative entertainment to the Broadway plays next door, and hucksters peddled watches and the apocalypse outside pizza parlors. Those were all just pieces of the panorama of opportunities and characters that made New York great.

I could walk those streets for hours, for years, and never get bored. Every block offered a stimulating new world, a promising adventure: Here's an old building with fanciful gargoyle gutters; there's a store overflowing with Indian imports. A supermodel walks past; a horn player you last saw in the Sun Ra Arkestra blows for change. A Mafioso was killed in this restaurant twenty years ago.

One day, my old college boyfriend Brian, who had moved from Providence to San Francisco to New York, and I walked from Park Slope in the middle of Brooklyn, down Flatbush Avenue, into the then raw and empty Dumbo area by the East River, across the Brooklyn Bridge, past City Hall, Chinatown, and the Lower East Side, to the East Village, my primary New York home. The sky was blue, the sun gentle. We grazed on ethnic delicacies, shops inflamed and inspired us with their racks of goods, and our feet begged for an Epsom salt soaking by the time the soft light of sunset painted the buildings red and pink.

The subways were the sites of daily odysseys too, not dulling commutes. Forget burrowing my head inside a newspaper (though the *New York Times* soon became an essential part of my New York love affair): I people-watched until my eyes ached. Sometimes, I would just look at feet, reading what the style and wear of riders' shoes said about their origins, journeys, and destinations. Other times, I compared noses, trying to guess ethnicities from shapes, bumps, and tips. (I had learned semiotics after all, to find in all things a text.) Once I watched a man whose one deformed eye stayed open as he slept; denied closure, the orb rolled grotesquely in its socket, chasing dream phantoms. I remember seeing a young family tear hungrily through a foul-smelling box of fried chicken. When they left, an Indian man across the aisle looked at me and shook his head sadly.

The parks housed human passion plays too, and gave you a chance to breathe tree-filtered air. There was a community garden with a turtle pond on Houston and Bowery, where I would read the Sunday *Times* and jot thoughts in my journal. Central Park was its own world. I wanted to give up rock 'n' roll and just be the park's beat reporter, explore its nooks and tell its denizens' stories. The carousel. The zoo. The observatory. The pool. The reservoir. Shakespeare. Summerstage. The toy-boat pond. The Frisbee green. Baseball diamonds. Bike riding. The disco roller skaters. The lake. The caricaturists. The stables. Gay cruising in the Ramble. Strawberry Fields. The Metropolitan Museum of Art. Ice skating. Break dancing. Iguanas on leashes. Dogs. Two buskers: one on sax, one on accordion, playing ragtime and vaudeville, rewinding history with their chant, "One more time!" An old codger pedaling his bike with a boom box in the basket, blaring "New York, New York."

The bars, the restaurants, the museums, the stores, the clubs: You could do something new in New York every day of your life and still learn only the basics of the city. And during that lifetime, half the things would have changed; others, like the buildings, would stay as they had for centuries.

Here was my infinity.

For several months, Jeff and I were two kids in love in the big city. He would sign up for an open mike at a bar off Tompkins

Square Park. The night was the center of what became known as the antifolk scene. I remember being awed by the Dylanesque virtuosity of one tow-headed musician there; I swear it was a yet unknown Beck. Late at night, the R train ran very sporadically, so sometimes Jeff and I would sit in the station waiting forever, but it was okay—we'd lean against each other and close our eyes.

We'd go to museums and art openings together, sucking in culture. We were poor, struggling to do what we wanted to, taking related jobs to pay the bills. I copyedited and scrounged for freelance writing gigs. Jeff did graphic design and tried to establish a career as an illustrator. On good nights, we ate at the Thai restaurant around the corner from our house. We tried not to venture the other direction, to the treeless blocks of grim projects and cars with no tires. We didn't live in the cool part of Long Island City, the area near Astoria where artists were congregating. There was little of interest in our neighborhood, not even good diners. The R was the only train nearby. Too often, it didn't run, and I would spend money I couldn't afford on a taxi.

I was sweet on my artist with the giant smile. He was cute, talented, good. But the more time I spent in New York, the more distracted from our relationship I became. Probably, I had trouble with commitment, with taking a relationship to the level past passion and comfort. Jeff and I had moved in together as much out of convenience as love. Prior to that, we hadn't even lived in the same town for the less than a year we'd been dating. Slowly, stealthily, like an accomplished adulterer weaving its web, the city sensed my weakness and conspired to steal me away. With all these options in front of me, a smorgasbord of romance, I just couldn't settle down.

Then, fate delivered me my own 512-square-foot slice of heaven.

A tip from a *Billboard* editor led me to East 5th Street. A barely affordable sublet in the Village sounded too good to be true. When I got to the building, I realized I knew the block well: I was ringing a doorbell at a big red tenement that was an identical twin, except for its hue, to its next-door neighbor, Big Pink.

Apartment six in Big Red was a shitty little railroad flat. The floors slanted six inches in the ten feet from one side to the other and were covered in stained, snot-colored carpet, except in the kitchen, whose dirty linoleum was cracked and peeling. The list of the floor made you feel like you were always drunk, falling into the walls. A glorified closet, the bathroom barely fit a tub and toilet. You had to wash your hands and face at the kitchen sink. At least the tub wasn't in the kitchen, as it was in so many East Village flats.

Big Red was a typical nineteenth-century, five-story tenement building. The furnace went out a lot. When it did work, the kitchen would be so hot I had to leave a window cracked. The electricity apparently hadn't been updated since it was first installed. You couldn't run too many other appliances if the window-unit air conditioner was on, or the power would blow. That unit only cooled half the apartment, barely, which was another reason I rarely cooked. No sunlight reached the interior since Big Red was built before building code reforms required airshafts. I had perpetual sinus infections from a century's buildup of mold and dust and the dry heat of steam radiators. Small wonder tenements are synonymous with tuberculosis.

But compared to my friends' studios, the four, tiny, doorless rooms I called home were a veritable Taj Mahal. Mostly, Big Red had that crucial real estate component: location, location, location. Open to car traffic for only two blocks, East 5th was quiet and tree lined, like a street in Brooklyn. An extra dose of sunlight hit the buildings directly across from my living room windows at day's end — hence, those sunset mauves and maroons, the colors of bricks brushed with evening light.

Contrary to everything I'd ever heard about New Yorkers, the people of East 5th were friendlier than neighbors I'd had in Beloit or Providence. I got my hair cut at the salon across the street. The block bars, Scratcher and Fish, were my second and third living rooms. My friend Jackie in the ground floor of Big Pink made me my first pair of leather pants. Neighbors and I cooked dinners together, loaned each other corkscrews, borrowed each other's showers when the water went out, carried each other home when we passed out at Scratcher. Even if we only nodded as we passed in the stairs or by the mailboxes, we knew each other. We watched as lovers and spouses came and went. We were neighbors, more constant than romances.

History is never far away in New York. Big Red was a block from Cooper Union, the arts college in whose Great Hall Abraham Lincoln once spoke. One day Bill Clinton followed in the Great Orator's footsteps. My friend Silver and I, presidential groupies, waited in the crowd outside. He grabbed her hand, said hello, his eyes lingering on her face. (Me, he ignored.)

Next door was Mother's, a storied film and TV studio where, in its '50s heyday, *The Honeymooners* was taped. I saw rapper Heavy

D shooting a video there once, watched Mark Pennington film John Leguizamo for the PBS series *The United States of Poetry*. In 1991, Mother's was gutted by a fire. Now, naturally, the building houses condos.

The street was a setting for celluloid fantasies. The police department on the next block provided the façade of the precinct headquarters in *NYPD Blue*. Spike Lee took over our block for a few weeks when he was shooting his film *Girl 6*. The heroine's apartment was directly across the street from mine. Camera operators stood on cranes outside my window and discreetly waved hello. For one scene, Lee strung hundreds of handheld receivers from old-fashioned desk phones on a cable across the street, then let them all fall at once. In the film, the rain of colorful plastic happens in slow motion. In real life, the fall was quick and cacophonous.

Famous people walked by all the time. I would run into Lenny Kaye, Patti Smith's right-hand man, on the corner; by the mid-'90s, I was friendly with the long-haired guitar hero. Before he died, the poet Allen Ginsberg was always around. Quentin Crisp, who wrote *The Naked Civil Servant*, was an unmistakable neighborhood presence with his carefully combed head of white hair. I would bask in his dignified, dandy presence at the corner diner, until he passed away in '99. Cool, indie-rock-loving comedian and actress Janeane Garofalo hung out at Scratcher, as did filmmaker Todd Solondz. Sometimes, I still see Sue Laguna, the model who clacked overhead in high heels in the apartment above me, in TV commercials.

Reading *How I Became Hettie Jones*, an autobiography by the ex-wife of Beat-era poet Leroi Jones (a.k.a. Amiri Baraka), I realized that Hettie was the little lady I sometimes saw walking down the street. She lived on the corner of my block, as she had since the '60s. We became friends; one day we had tea in her rooftop garden. I loved her story of a bohemian woman's unbeaten path, of her efforts to raise two daughters on a poet's meager pay. The scene where she struggles to push a carriage and bag of laundry down East Village streets, cursing the artist fathers who obliviously avoid such travails, is burned into my brain.

In 1989, the East Village was *the* New York place to be if you were young, hungry for music, film, art, or poetry, and desperately seeking good, cheap food and a place to lay your head. The area was rapidly gentrifying; still, you didn't have to walk far to find drugs and prostitutes keeping the yuppies at bay. I could go to a dozen clubs a night, see hot bands, and never leave my 'hood. The area was transitioning from an ethnic enclave to an artistic one; the changeover wasn't happening peacefully. Tompkins Square Park was the battlefield. Reagan's army of the homeless had taken up residence and was not about to skedaddle so that boomers could walk dogs and push strollers. Besides, where could they go? The neighborhood's numerous anarchists took up the destitutes' cause. A couple months after I moved to East 5th, a squatter band called Missing Foundation ended a concert in the park with a performance riot, featuring the de rigueur bonfire, banging of sheet metal, throwing of bottles, and taunting of police. It was Watts as rock opera. This time, the cops didn't take the bait.

I met up that night with two short-haired, pale-faced, young anarchists who had recently fled Eastern Europe. We sat on the square's benches and drank beers hidden in paper bags. One nocturnal park resident came up and gave us his review of the show, in which he drew on the ancient myths of his Native American tribe. The night, the park, the time was all about the displaced, this place that was disappearing.

The punk boys were virtually homeless, too. I brought the younger one back to Big Red with me, just for one night. My time with Jeff was over.

Jeff wrote a song about me. "The Last Day" painted nowhere near as pretty a picture as "Natural High" had. In Velvets-esque raw blues, the song mourned my indifference when we broke up, my heartlessness, the ease with which I had moved on and left my love feeling used.

By that time, I had found my first community of friends and thinkers. I moved from copyediting at *Billboard* to copyediting at the *Village Voice*. The tabloid of downtown was one of the last bastions for progressive voices. At a time when other weeklies were avoiding politics to peg their fortunes on "lifestyle" and magazines were slipping into the star-fucker abyss from which they have yet to emerge, the *Voice* managed to make New Journalism seem not vintage but vital. *Rolling Stone* was pandering to yuppies, *Vanity Fair* was sucking celebrity dick, *The New Yorker* hadn't cared about pop culture since Ellen Willis left in the '70s, and *Creem* was locked in an eternal Ouija board search for Lester Bangs' soul. The *Voice* could be cranky and predictable, but it was also where you'd find a young woman (Kathy Dobie) infiltrating the Right to Life movement and writing an empathic, complicated, must-read epic that set new standards for what participatory journalism could be.

In terms of rock criticism, the *Voice* set the pace for the field. It was a place where controversial takes on landmark records were announced and denounced in critical pissing matches, neologisms ("rockist," "postrock," "pigfucker music" as Robert Christgau dubbed Jon Spencer et al.) were coined, and new writers were nurtured. The *Voice* was also where recent Yale graduates competed to write the most jargon-ridden, inscrutable, metatextual deconstructions of obscure records, thus alienating music lovers by the legions. I preferred critics' pith, such as the writer who responded to Bobby McFerrin's a cappella hit "Don't Worry Be Happy" with a succinct "Fuck you."

The *Voice's* sheer scope made it a writer's paradise. Its pages covered politics, fashion, books, TV, the media, dance, sports. Giants of their specialties roamed the office: passionate civil rights defender Nat Hentoff, media critic Geoffrey Stokes, edgy art sleuth C. Carr, hip-hop aesthete Greg Tate, film philosopher J. Hoberman. Old-school rock critic Ellen Willis coined the term "pro-sex feminism" in the *Voice*, launching a legion of followers like myself. Richard Goldstein pushed the envelope of post-Stonewall queer thought. Michael Musto penned trenchant social criticism disguised as gossip columns.

All those articles came through the copy department. At times, I felt like I was getting the best schooling I'd ever had, and getting paid to boot. We bottom-feeders were cocky enough to argue among ourselves, and even with the authors, about our great writers' takes. The quality of intellectual debate was manna to my hungry brain. Sometimes, the distance between our hotly pursued ideas and most people's lived reality tugged at my conscience; what good was debate over the authenticity of Bon Jovi to my old classmates in Beloit, struggling to find jobs as factories closed. Too much pretension was likely to get knocked down by a well-placed sarcastic jibe or prank. When Brian moved to New York and joined our little debate team, his dry wit fit right in.

My fellow copy editors became my best friends and lovers. Kathy and I would talk five times a day to hash out everything: world events, outfits, music, sex. A dark-haired knockout from Boston, men had trouble seeing past her magnificent breasts to her brains. But there was tragedy behind her beauty: Kathy had broken her neck in a car crash a few years before we met. When she talked about how she lay by the side of the road thinking it was important that she not move, or about how she sat alone in the cafeteria at Harvard in her neck brace as students skirted her like a freak, small tears would run nobly down her face. (Me, my face got all red and scrunchy when I cried.) Kathy miraculously recovered with no paralysis, but after that, she gave up drinking and drugs. Dating female rock stars and male academic luminaries, she had the kind of love life I could only sigh at and admire. But that was okay, because several months after my breakup with Jeff, I started seeing Ed.

Eight years older than me, Ed was a native New Yorker, born and raised in the Bronx. He, too, had felt slightly out of place as an undergraduate at a private New England liberal arts college. Both his parents were born in Puerto Rico. I was woefully ignorant of Latin culture, and he was my patient teacher. We saw Tito Puente, Celia Cruz, Danilo Pérez, Michel Camilo, Rubén Blades, Willie Colón. He showed me the New York that he knew like the back of his hand, from its outerborough neighborhoods to its downtown art scenes. Ed had that jaundiced New Yorker savvy about everything; from hip-hop to performance art to squatter punk to beatnik literature, there was little he didn't know about or hadn't seen.

And yet, he seemed a little left out of it all, as if the happenings had rolled by this son of a transit worker and left him on the platform, swaying in the breeze.

We rode our bikes through Central Park, ate pierogis for breakfast at East Village Ukrainian diners, went to the Latin jazz night at the Village Gate, and checked out the latest Kurosawa film at the Angelika Film Center. But mostly, we hung out at the Nuyorican Poets Café.

The Nuyorican had been a home for the Latin arts movement of the '70s, fostering such writers as Miguel Algarín, Miguel Piñero, Piri Thomas, Pedro Pietri, and Bimbo Rivas. Like most good things in life, it disappeared in the '80s, then was reborn in '89 in a Lower East Side tenement. Run by a board of five somewhat cantankerous writers, including Algarín and the charismatic Bob Holman, the Nuyorican became the center of a literary uprising. I found there the sort of vibrant, diverse, intellectual, creative maelstrom I'd always dreamed of diving into. Ed became one of the Nuyorican's poets. And I became the scene's chronicler, covering "the new poetry" for the *Voice*, *Rolling Stone*, and *Ms*.

We were all Nuyoricans: That was the open, inclusive, revolutionary embrace of the café and its surrounding scene. "Nuyorican meant poetry for the people, by the people," Algarín told me in 1991, explaining the evolution of a word that he first heard used as an epithet for Puerto Ricans from New York when he and his friends got off a plane in San Juan. It became the name of a 1970s anthology, then a café, then a scene. The Nuyorican symbolized an era that celebrated people coming together, not the tribalism of identity politics, as some jealous academics and media playa-haters would eventually misconstrue the scene. Playwright and master heckler Steve Cannon called his magazine *The Gathering of the Tribes*; the local bookstore was named Mosaic.

I found myself immersed in a galaxy of creative types who, like me, had felt beaten down in the '80s and now, as walls and governments crashed down around the world, were crawling out of their hiding places. We were sharing the thoughts we had kept secret, our hopes, scribbled dreams, and nightmares. Poems were like calls to arms: "You know things! Think them!" Holman shouted, quoting fellow poet Mike Tyler, in "1990," the exploding, inevitable epic that became a Nuyorican greatest hit. The good poets competed not simply to win the weekly poetry slam but to challenge each other with a new work every week. Brains buzzed. Inspired one night, I sat at a café table and began scribbling down a list of ideas.

"The idealists! That's what we can call ourselves," I told Ed. "Our manifestos will be idea lists."

I was anxious to be part of a movement, to go down in history books along with the constructivists, surrealists, Beats, abstract expressionists, hippies, and punks. The Nuyorican epitomized New York for me: explosive, multicultural, bursting with talent, a little inebriated, a little more horny, on the make, on the edge, and endlessly amusing.

"I go downtown, I walk alone, This city's my home, I'm not alone in my home." Jean Smith used to wander through clubs on Mecca Normal's tours of America and sing this four-line anthem as a form of not-mute protest. Her city is Vancouver, but she was taking back the night for women everywhere, claiming "the right to walk wherever the fuck I choose," as she'd say when she introduced the song.

In all my big-city wanderings, at every hour of the night and day, I was never mugged or raped. Once, while I was distracted by carrying a giant bouquet of discarded lilies, a pickpocket slipped my wallet out of my backpack. Another time, I was walking through the West Village after a late movie, and a student type, probably from New Jersey, pushed me up against a wall and proceeded to mumble what he'd like to do to me, his alcohol breath in my face. His friends pulled him off me, and, heart pounding, I made it home.

Both incidents were minor threats compared to the slow psychic death I would have suffered those dozen years if I had driven the same strip-mall-lined route to and from an office in an air-conditioned car, watching TV at night and getting retail therapy at Wal-Mart.

New York is Shangri-la for independent women. Yoko Ono knew this (that's why she wrote a song called "New York Woman"), Patti Smith fled the "Piss Factory" for CBGB's, Madonna fell into downtown's groove, and *Sex and the City* made the geographic tryst a sitcom for the world. New York doesn't judge you if you're unmarried, child free, and career obsessed; if you like walking down the street in a slip, eating out every meal, staying in clubs all night, and having sex with strangers; if you want to spend a work day visiting museums and staring in shop windows. Of course you can do those things. Maybe, you should do them.

In her 1929 seminal work about women writers, *A Room of One's Own*, Virginia Woolf wrote, "Intellectual freedom depends upon material things. Poetry depends upon intellectual freedom. And women have always been poor, not for two hundred years merely, but from the beginning of time. Women have had less intellectual freedom than the sons of Athenian slaves. Women, then, have not had a dog's chance of writing poetry. That is why I have laid so much stress on money and a room of one's own."

Like a frontier woman staking out her territory, I set up camp in Big Red. First, Brendalyn, my truest, bestest friend, was my roommate; when she died one terrible summer night, it took two cats— whom, in a Kathy Acker moment, I dubbed God and Elvis—to replace her. That aging apartment with its cracked linoleum became my sanctuary, my laboratory, my piece of paradise, sometimes my hell. I had not one, but four, rooms of my own. In New York I developed, sometimes with great difficulty, a career, a source of "material things." And I even wrote poetry.

In Beloit and at Brown, isolation had been thrust upon me. In New York, I often chose to be alone, but I was rarely lonely. Any time I needed to be around human beings, they were easy to find. Bars stayed open until 4 a.m. The infamous Russian restaurant Kiev, twenty-four-hour hangout of club hoppers fueling up on carbohydrates, was two blocks from the East Village apartment that was my palace for a dozen years. Or I could just sit on my stoop and watch the city roll by.

5

No Martyrs

⚬ ⚬ ⚬

During my first summer in Big Red, my mother came to New York. Her frequent visits over the years have blurred together into a montage of museums, shops, shows, and meals. I don't remember everything we did that particular day. Probably, we caught a musical. I gladly suffered through *Cats* and *Les Misérables* in order to spend an afternoon with Mom.

I do remember dinner. It wasn't the kind of meal one forgets.

Compared to the neighboring Ukrainian diners and vegetarian cafés, Miracle Grill was upscale. The backyard dining area was an unlikely oasis between crumbling brick tenements. Oil lamps lit stone walkways, and trees helped muffle street noise. The food was excellent but not pretentious: hearty Tex-Mex steaks and frozen margaritas. Over fresh salsa and blue chips, Mom and I talked like girlfriends. It was the first heart to heart we'd had in years, the first time I didn't feel like she was judging or lecturing me.

Mom could tell I was doing well, although, freshly broken up with Jeff, I was lovelorn. My career was taking off. I was writing for a few publications, some of which she had even heard of. Big Red impressed her, despite the wine-stained carpet. Mom was happy for me. In a way, I was embarking on the kind of life she had always wanted.

Born in Kentucky, my mother was the youngest of six children, the only one to get a high school degree. Her father, a skilled builder and World War I veteran with a serious drinking problem, eventually moved the family to Los Angeles.

Mom had overcome the hardships of a sometimes precarious upbringing to become my feminist role model. Politically liberal, but rather conservative socially (I think life wound up changing that a bit), she was a woman caught in and helping to reroute the mainstream: a professional, a wife, a mother. She dressed tastefully, handsomely, in pantsuits or A-line skirts with sensible heels. It was Dad who objected when I shaved my legs, not she. She fought against my wildness, my embrace of sex, drugs, and rock 'n' roll—she approved only of the latter. We clashed hard when I was a teen. One day, she slapped me for sassing back. I slapped her in return.

Mom was always big on humanist issues, like civil rights and feminism. She lived the shift in women's power away from the home; it saved her life. She deservedly valued her career and her brain and didn't play second fiddle to Dad. In fact, she earned more than he (a fact he often pointed out with more pride than embarrassment). Brett and I were latchkey kids. Babysitters watched over us in the hours between the end of school and my parents' workday.

Still, when Mom came home, she fell into a traditional role, cooking, cleaning, helping the kids with their homework, neglecting herself. She's of that era of mothers who are young-fashioned

enough to be aware that they were making sacrifices, but old-fashioned enough that they went ahead and made them—the martyr
generation. Although she was the one who excelled in college and
made Phi Beta Kappa (again, something Dad bragged about more
than she did), it was Dad who got the Ph.D. Mom typed up his
and her master's theses while the first pains of labor were hitting,
then went to Glendale Memorial and had Brett. These are the stories I've heard again and again.

When Dad moved east to teach, Mom followed. Except for
Mama, we didn't have a nanny. Some years, a housekeeper came
once a week. Both my parents are neatniks, and they kept the
house spotless, despite being a two-career couple. In retrospect, as
I try to stay on top of my pigpile pen, I don't know how they did it.

Maybe it's just a daughter's blind love, but I think Mom could
have been "someone": a writer, scholar, actress. Having studied
and lived its contradictions and promises, she has a vast understanding of, and deep feel for, American culture. I always turn to
her for perspective on world issues. It was Mom I called, sobbing,
after I first turned on the TV on September 11, 2001. For once,
she had no wisdom to offer.

Mom was an award-winning, much-loved, and highly respected
teacher. She raised two kids. She *was* someone. But I always felt
like she wanted more. She would frequently tell me as much.
Don't sell yourself short, she would warn. Don't let love get in the
way of the rest of your life. Think for yourself. Support yourself.
Don't marry the first guy you fall in love with. Live with him first
rather than make a mistake. Wait to have kids.

Mom herself waited until her late twenties to have us. She told
me only recently that the delay was in part caused by the difficulties

of her early married days, when she didn't know how, or if, the relationship would last. Coming from a family of six, being childless for that long must have made her feel both rebellious and ashamed. She was an in-betweener too, trapped between two eras: the age of June Cleaver and that of Gloria Steinem. She knew the one wasn't the role model for her, but the second wasn't yet lighting a new path.

At Miracle Grill that summer night, Mom and I were talking about relationships. She had never been much for boy talk. Shy and awkward as a youth, she didn't date a lot before meeting Dad. Her advice on relationships had always been statistical, the kind she gave her social studies students: the percentage of marriages that worked when the couple lived together before getting married versus after, the effect of divorce on children's self-esteem, and so forth. She wasn't the kind of mom who sat on the bed and regaled me with stories of her early romantic missteps or instructed me on the pleasures and importance of the female orgasm.

She was a pragmatist; I was a romantic. I remember, as a kid, showing her what must have been my first poem, in which I compared love to a river that shoots through rapids and hurtles down waterfalls, before ending in a pool in paradise.

Mom read it carefully. Twice. Then, she looked at me strangely. Her blue eyes were outlined in red, as they often were (we eventually figured out she was allergic to my cats).

"It's very nice dear," she said in a rather odd tone. "But do you really think that's what marriage brings: happily ever after?"

Yes, I wanted to answer. Isn't that what all those Disney movies you take us to teach? Isn't that what happens after Prince Charming kisses and wakes the princess and everything fades to black? After every wedding scene since the dawn of romantic comedy?

Judging by the inflection in Mom's voice, I realized the answer was no.

Mom couldn't douse my heart. You couldn't listen to as many pop songs as I have and not be in love with love. Even when my turntable mocked it ("Love Will Tear Us Apart") and mourned it ("You've Got to Hide Your Love Away"), love—the search for my one, true life partner, my Platonic missing half—was a preoccupation. I held on to Vince because we had said those fateful words to each other—I love you—and that was supposed to bind our souls. Every time I said those words—I love you—to every subsequent lover, husband, and friend, I clung to them as if they were written in stone. Still, despite my best intentions, my heart slowly began to suspect that it was another body organ saying, "I love you." Eventually, I realized the words were a cover, because "I love you" would transform sex (anxiety causing, guilt provoking, possibly dangerous, not condoned by Mom) into making love (noble, sensual, heroic, fun).

Dating was a huge part of college life. But relationships were sort of like classes: you shopped around your first couple years and tried out new subjects. By junior year, you had to make a commitment to a field, though you could still fool around on the side if you lusted after an ambitious course load. Your concentration didn't necessarily have anything to do with what you would do after you graduated; you might just look back on it as something you were interested in during your experimental youth. I don't know anyone who wound up with his or her college amour. Wanda and I talked the boy talk plenty, but we sure as hell weren't ready to walk that walk down the aisle.

Then, the week after our graduation from Brown, a *Newsweek* cover story, "The Marriage Crunch" announced that if women were still single at thirty, they had only a 20 percent chance of ever getting married. If they hadn't gotten hitched by forty, they had more chances of getting killed by a terrorist than finding a life partner, the article infamously, tackily said. Supposedly based on "scientific" studies, the data seemed suspect. Still, to those of us who were just entering the workforce, the report was like a mass-media-disseminated confirmation of our worst fears, a cosmic threat letter: Go ahead, put your career first, don't focus on starting a family, and enjoy your spinster old age!

Wanda, who had moved with Janice to Washington, D.C., to work as a legislative aide while I was spinning wheels and records in Providence, in particular was suddenly consumed with the issue of the marriage crunch. "Don't you think men can smell desperation on you?" she worried in one phone conversation, scolding me for my apathy about nest building.

I wondered what desperation smelled like. I imagined a toxic cocktail of cat piss, the burning wires of an overused vibrator, dusty romance novels, vinegary red wine, and frustrated pheromones. Eww.

Still, the *Newsweek* article and others like it threw a fist in the girl-go-getter's esophagus. The notion that the price for our chosen independence would be a lifetime of loneliness caused the first generation of women raised on free choice, girls' softball, and *Ms.* magazine to question the gains our mothers had won for us. We weren't ready to have babies. But we didn't want our unreadiness now to keep us from ever having a family, someday, down the road.

(In retrospect, that fear-mongering study was another scare tactic in an '80s phenomenon that Susan Faludi described in her landmark book, *Backlash: The Undeclared War against American Women*. News stories like these circulated as part of a right-wing sabotage effort aimed at undermining women's baby steps toward liberation. Twenty years later, in fact, in another cover story, *Newsweek* recanted "The Marriage Crunch," admitting what I and scores of other women had already proved wrong.)

Even if you were throwing your whole body into the resistance against the so-called Moral Majority, it was hard not to feel the pressure to marry and breed. Patti Smith herself was doing it, locked away with her guitarist husband, Fred Sonic Smith, in a Detroit suburb, making babies Jesse and Jackson. (At least when she poked her head out, she was still righteous, singing, "People Have the Power.")

And then there was the sledgehammer blow AIDS delivered to the idea of free love. The '80s threw a lubricated (not the same as wet) rubber blanket over the long, soft-core seduction of the '70s.

Armed inadequately with the tools of deconstruction, our generation groped through the tangle of mixed messages about sex and love. We came up with our own compromise between deadly debauches and the shackles of matrimony: serial monogamy. My friends and I went from one serious relationship to another. After Vince came Paul, then Ethan, then Brian, then Jeff, then Ed. We weren't marrying, but we weren't not marrying. Like kids playing house, we practiced marriage, and hoped and prayed that practice would make perfect.

Mom and I were two liberated, career-oriented women meeting in that city garden setting, on that lovely summer day in the late '80s. But love was on our minds.

"I seem to just get bored with men," I said to Mom. "Or else, they break my heart. I don't know if it's them or me. I love Jeff. I thought I was in love with him. But I've thought that a half-dozen times before, and now I don't know if I even know what 'in love' means, if I believe in love at all."

"Why does it always have to be about love? Can't you just enjoy men's companionship, without worrying over whether they're 'the one,'" Mom asked. "I'm worried that you're spending so much time worrying about love, when you should be focusing on your career. What's your hurry?"

"You know what those studies say. If I don't find a man by the time I'm twenty-five, am I going to end up a spinster? And is that such a bad thing? How did you know that you loved Dad? And how do you stay in love, all these years?"

Mom's eyes were blue marbles on red spiderwebs dripping with tears. She could barely talk.

"We don't, honey," she said.

And then there was a long pause until she could speak again.

"Your dad wanted me to wait to tell you this. He wanted us to tell you together, but I think you need to know now. We've decided to get a divorce."

I never fooled myself that my parents' relationship was perfect. But it seemed pretty good. We spent numerous summers all crammed together in trailers and never came close to killing each other. We ate dinner together every night, albeit with the TV news on or everyone hunched over whatever they were reading. We sat in the living room and watched *M*A*S*H, All in the Family, Maude.* We went to movies and plays, shared books, canoed, and traveled to Europe.

For all our genuine closeness, we were also the kind of family that kept things inside. Sometimes, I could sense hostility, coldness, between Mom and Dad. Frequently, I was the pressure valve through which tension escaped. Fighting over homework one night when I was way too young to be using that kind of language, I called my dad a fucking asshole. "See, that's the attitude they think they can get away with," he said to Mom, more injured than angry. Instead of giving me the spanking I deserved, he fled alone to their room. Dad had an inferiority complex. He thought Mom was on a pedestal, teaching us to look down on him. Maybe there was something to that. But, really, I think I thought I could call him a fucking asshole because it was he who looked down on himself.

By high school, the pressure was exploding. Unbeknownst to us kids, Dad's drinking was giving him trouble at work and in his marriage. And I was shooting off everywhere, looking for love in the wrong arms, smoking pot, hurting myself. Senior year, I went to a psychologist, who told me my troubles were not just my own; they were my parents'. They joined me in counseling. Grievances were aired. Smoke cleared.

Still, as with so many couples, once their kids had fled the nest, my parents' reasons for staying together evaporated. When I came home from college for vacations, they snapped at each other constantly. At my graduation, Dad walked out of a dinner the Raifords and I were hosting and disappeared for hours. My parents seemed to be doing things separately more and more: Mom traveling with her fellowships, Dad involved in teacher-education organizations that took him to conferences around the country. On separate occasions, he took Brett and me out for dinner when he was nearby for a meeting. A colleague of his, an even-tempered woman named Judy, joined us. A few years later, she became Dad's wife.

Bad news hits as abstraction. My parents are divorcing, I thought. They are joining that growing statistic. I am now the daughter of a broken home. Wow, real drama!

Part of me was relieved at the prospect of having my parents separate, but happy, rather than together and miserable. I was certainly tired of living under the burden of the latter. Eventually, we would all achieve the former.

The hardest part was how divorce hurt Mom. My beloved heroine took the end of her marriage as an immense failure. After all, her mother had put up with her asshole dad all those years. Mom may have been the only one of her siblings to get a high-school diploma, but she was also the first to get a divorce. For all her independence, she believed strongly in family. She taught a course in family planning. She knew well the high toll divorce could take on children. Probably, that's why she waited so long.

Watching a parent suffer is a terrible thing. Your positions are thrown into reverse: You now comfort the one who has always taken care of you, the person on whom you have relied as your pillar of competence, assurance, and strength. I never thought I would have to counsel my mother through a broken heart. I was the one who was always making the stupid love choices (as she inevitably recognized first); she was the one who had it infinitely to-gether. I had never seen my mother so broken down in tears, so helpless, as I did in the first years after her divorce.

"Did I waste all that time?" she would wonder about the thirty-two years of her marriage. "What's the point of having come this far only to wind up apart?"

I didn't have an answer, except I thought Brett and I were proof that the years weren't a waste (as Dad would tell her, as she, too, would admit).

My parents' divorce broke my heart, yet it also made me feel less alone. The silence in our far-flung house was shattered. We could talk of our troubles. Mom and I even discussed sex.

I'm grateful Brett and I were spared the confusion and agony of being raised by divorced parents. I'm sure we are less scarred than we would have been if we had had to cope with our parents' fight-ing over furniture while we were still too young to ride our bikes to town. Sure, I would prefer it if, for the rest of my adult life, I didn't have to navigate the touchy shoals of deciding which parent to spend which holiday with or to act as messenger service between them ("Mom, Dad says that if you want to sell the California prop-erty . . . "). If we could all be happy driving a trailer across 1970s America together again, I'd do it in a minute.

But them days are gone.

Divorce didn't make me give up on love. But I did understand why Mom threw that big rock in my prepubescent poetic pool. I don't know if the troubles that upset my parents' marriage in their first years never went away, if they were just pushed deep below the surface by the needs and distractions of raising a family. It seems like we had years of floating happily in that pool, disturbed by occasional wavy patches. Maybe living through my parents' inability to stay connected has undermined my own faith in fidelity. Watching my parents' marriage fall apart didn't stop my own first union from failing.

I did learn one thing from Mom, sometimes inadvertently. It was summarized by a T-shirt I saw a woman wearing in 1994 at the Michigan Womyn's Music Festival, that petri dish gathering of feminism in action. Amid all the bare breasts, purple tie-dye, and black leather was a plain white shirt emblazoned with the word "martyrs," with a circle around it and a slash through it. No martyrs. That was the lesson Mom taught: Don't be a martyr. Don't throw yourself on your husband's funeral pyre; don't be Joan of Fucking Arc dead; don't be a doormat.

That doesn't necessarily mean don't sacrifice. You don't have to replace selflessness with selfishness. Sometimes, for love, you have to surrender a little bit.

Just don't give yourself away.

6

The Gay '90s

◑ ◑ ◑

It's a fairy tale: While on vacation in a European city, you meet a tall, dark, and handsome man. Together, you visit museums, castles, and nightclubs, stroll alongside rivers and down famous streets, and make the tender, passionate love you've been dreaming about for at least a dozen years. You're in love, for the first, last, and always time. You move to exotic parts of the world together: Taiwan, San Francisco. You pledge your devotion and slip a ring on each other's fingers in front of a wildly supportive crowd. You live happily ever after—or at least fifteen years and counting.

It happened, it really happened: to my brother.

On February 14, 1992, three years after our parents' thirty-two-year marriage dissolved, I watched Brett "wed" his boyfriend, Paul, at San Francisco's city hall. It was the one-year anniversary of the city's enactment of a landmark domestic-partnership law. Since in San Francisco you can't spit without turning expectoration into a performance-art-happening-cum-political-protest, activists organized a mass wedding to celebrate. Brett and Paul were one of hundreds of rabble-rousing, hand-holding couples making a statement about rights and visibility, as well as love. Couples cried and cheered. My brothers, as I came to call them, kissed and hugged. The ceremony wasn't something for which they'd sent out embossed invitations. But since I'd interrupted my East Village idyll with a year in San Francisco, I came with a bouquet, a flower girl in flower-child land. It was the best Valentine's Day ever.

But it was just one day. Adventure and a job brought me for a dozen months to the city where being an outsider makes you an insider, wondering where I belonged.

In the early '90s, the gay '90s, San Francisco was the place to be. The city's alternative bent had its roots in the wild and wooly Barbary Coast and was sealed with a wet, bong-tasting kiss in the 1960s. It was the coolest, weirdest, raddest place in America—and one of the most beautiful, with its hills with gingerbread houses poking out of the fog, bridges like necklaces strung across the bay, streetcars careening through Chinatown, and tattooed lesbians making glorious noise.

In '91, the Bay Area was only just starting to capitulate to the yuppie sellout—the tech and real estate boom—that had already ended the countercultural revolution everywhere else in America. San Francisco was still supposedly abundant with scenic, spacious Victorian apartments affordable enough to house legions of recent college graduates. The cheap rents facilitated the underemployment of the overeducated. Everyone had a project—a film, a band, a book, a club, a political party, a party party, a revolution—the stranger, the better. I knew people who collected driver's education crash films and those who made high-tech aural pornography. Brilliant eccentrics were everyday San Franciscans;

Armistead Maupin probably had to tone down real-life person-ages for his *Tales of the City*.

My roommate, who called herself Lala, was a musician and artist, a beautiful, dazed girl who had been medically certified in-sane enough to live off disability, a not uncommon Bay Area form of dole. She sang in a band/situationist ensemble called Caroliner Rainbow, led by a sweet, odd genius named Grux, who sometimes spent the night in the living room with Lala. They slept there un-der the streetlamps because Caroliner's props and costumes filled her tiny bedroom. The surreal, fluorescent concoctions of card-board and cloth were dozing puppets haunting our home, waiting for a spirit to move them.

I knew Lala because she had dated the drummer of one of the Minneapolis bands that used to crash in my Providence apartment. We had looked and looked but couldn't find one of those magic, cheap, giant flats everyone else seemed to have; they were being swallowed up by gentrification, San Francisco's edge disappearing in a money fog. Instead, we wound up with this awkwardly divided space—what had been the parlor floor of a single-family house now passed for a two-bedroom abode—on a sketchy, treeless block in an area with one of the highest crime rates in the city. Johns would troll me as I walked home from the train station. "I have glasses and a backpack," I wanted to shout at them. "Do I look like a whore?"

San Francisco had long been the number-one destination in my years and years of daydream-nation travel plans. California was where I saw myself settling—a place where I could see moun-tains, smell the ocean, go barefoot, and watch guys with long hair balance on hard boards, where everyone wasn't so East Coast up-tight or Midwest tight-lipped. When I moved to New York, I gave myself three years there, tops. I'd get some clips under my belt, make some high-level publishing contacts, then move back to my homeland and live on a ranch with a view of the Pacific and a pet cougar. Turns out I was exactly right—and all wrong.

First off, I fell for New York in a way I hadn't anticipated. The Nuyorican, Big Red, Ed, Kathy, Brian, the Village: I was happy. The only thing I didn't have—what everyone else came to New York for—was a job. The *Voice* kept promising me one, stringing me along as a freelance writer and copyeditor. I suffered the whims of the publishing economy when my assistant-editor gig at a young magazine called *Model* died after two months, along with the publication. I was writing for the *Voice*, *Billboard*, *Rolling Stone*, *Spin*, *Creem*, but the money was minimal and sporadic. Freelancing was fine if you had some other source of financial security, like a trust fund. Me, I just had worry as backup. "Do you have health insurance?" Dad would ask every time we talked. So I didn't call much.

Then, fate gave me its fickle finger. In the summer of '91, I heard the *SF Weekly* was looking for a music editor. I flew out for the interview, got the job, packed my stuff, and moved—three years almost to the day from my arrival in New York.

It was odd: For most New Yorkers, careers were plentiful and apartments scarce, but, me, I had great digs but no gig. In flat-happy, job-sad San Francisco, I was gainfully employed but poorly domiciled. I was rubbing against the zeitgeist, or maybe it was rubbing against me.

The best part about living in San Francisco was being five blocks from my brothers. Brett and I had always been close. All those summers spent jammed in a trailer, we had to be. He was the introvert; I, the party girl. As a kid, Brett liked to throw a football around and even play cowboys and Indians, but he only had a couple friends. By adolescence, he was mostly burying himself in books or hiding beneath headphones. He was quiet, studious, thoughtful. But he was always engaged with and interested in the world. He wasn't a loner or misanthrope. In fact, he was well regarded and respected. Brett has an absolute sense of integrity, justice, and loyalty that's both fearsome and inspiring. I've been told more than once that my brother is the nicest person in the world.

Brett never dated. Sometimes, I would tease him, try to find out if he was interested in some girl, what his "type" was. In junior high, he admitted to thinking a tough-chick, white-trash knockout named Jennifer was cute. I ruined that confession by relentlessly bugging him about it. He never breathed a word of sexual interest after that. If I asked, he would clam up, get mad, walk away.

It didn't take a rocket scientist to guess he was gay.

Equal rights for minorities, women, and atheists were absolute commandments in a liberal house like ours. But gay rights? Not so much. When Brett and I were kids, our aunt Helen left my dad's half-brother Hank and their two children. Our parents explained this family scandal in grave, hushed tones.

"Helen is a lesbian," they said. "Do you know what that is?"

"No."

"That means she has a woman, not a man, for a partner."

"And?"

And . . . nothing. I was outraged, not by Helen's sin and infidelity but by the fact that everyone was so shocked a woman would love another woman. From that point on, I was all for homosexuality. Gay rights became a little crusade of mine. In high school, I wrote reports on books about gay theory and history and took an inordinate interest in *The Rocky Horror Picture Show*. Whenever there was a discussion of civil liberties, I would pipe up and add sexual orientation to the list of discriminated groups who deserved equality. Maybe I was looking for a little shock value. I was definitely starting to realize this was an issue that was going to have special relevance in my life.

Around senior year, Brett began spending a lot of time with a friend he knew from orchestra class. Clayton was a large blond with a loud laugh and dramatic hand gestures. He tended to be tasteless and coarse, a bit of a self-styled, white-trash dandy with an affected Southern drawl and all—imagine Truman Capote as a boisterous giant. Clayton could also be a hoot, a button-pusher, a transgressive (and transvestite) daredevil. He certainly wasn't like any of Brett's other friends: fellow professor's sons with whom my brother mostly talked about books and records.

One day, Clayton came into my room for a little chat. He did that from time to time, when he got bored with quiet old Brett. This day, he seemed upset.

"Can I tell you something?" he said. "Brett doesn't want me to, but I think you should know."

Clayton acted like he wanted to confide, but the edge in his tone made me uncomfortable, like I was about to be used in a manipulation game.

"I think you should listen to Brett," I said.

"Don't side with your brother! You know he's too secretive. Now darling," and Clayton grabbed my hands. "You've probably figured this out, but I'm telling you straight—no pun intended, ha ha! Brett and I are more than just close friends . . . if you know what I mean." And he gave my hands a painful squeeze.

I knew, of course. But I didn't want to know. Not from someone else, in this manner that seemed hurt and hurtful, more vindictive than vindicating. Not from someone besides my brother. I tried to brush the moment off, play it off, get Clayton out of my room and my head, rewind and erase.

Not as pleased with himself as he thought he would be, my brother's big friend went to Brett's room. I reluctantly followed, and we stood in Brett's doorway.

"I told her," Clayton said.

"You did not." My brother looked at me and didn't look at me. Anger and embarrassment turned his face the color of his red bedspread, a red my color-blind sibling probably mistook for black. "You did not!" he shouted, then slammed his door shut.

Brett didn't come out (so to speak) for a long time.

I didn't bring the incident up again for years, never told my parents. Brett's sexual orientation was a nontopic in our house. Mom and Dad didn't push him to date, didn't pester him with questions—but they didn't go around praising homosexuality as a life option either. I tried to give my brother opportunities to talk to me, to let him know I was homophilic. While we were home from college for Christmas break one year, we went to Madison to see Hüsker Dü play. On the ride home, I told Brett that the singer Bob Mould was widely believed to be gay (several years later, Mould came out). "That's kind of cool, right?" I prodded. But Brett didn't take the bait, on that long Wisconsin night or ever.

Maybe, tormented with accepting and admitting his own desires, he didn't see what was so cool about being gay.

Brett went through college without dating. Then, he went to Cambridge, England, for graduate studies. Perhaps the separation of a sea gave him the comfort zone he needed to be himself. Or maybe it was just time.

I got a letter from him one day while I was at Brown. I was sitting in Paula Vogel's drama class, half-listening to a lecture on Beckett or Shepard or Ionesco or, most poetically, perhaps Tennessee Williams, when I read about how Brett had gone to Berlin. There, he had met an American named Paul, whom he liked very much. So much, that he was in the process of coming out of the closet as a gay man. This letter, he wrote, in typically arch meta-confession for my brainy bro', was part of that process.

I not only connected with my brothers in San Francisco: I found a sisterhood.

In Providence and New York, I had quickly discovered that anatomical differences made me an oddity even in the oddball world of rock critics. Almost all my peers, role models, gatekeepers, and check payers were male. On good days, my tomboy soul was just fine with interviewing boys in bands, talking about bands with boys, comparing collections of records like they were baseball cards, and getting sound advice from paternalistic elders. I felt like I was back on Turtle Ridge again, playing Capture the Flag with the gang.

But the bad days—which, paradoxically, seemed to become more common, the more successful I got—were like that fateful bike ride in junior high. I realized that I was an outsider with no key to the boys' club door and no vote in making the clubhouse rules. When the door was shut, I was left lonely outside. And hungry and cold.

On the Left Coast, it was better. There was no eastern seaboard establishment to mirror. It was the real New World, still a frontier, a place for pioneer gals. There were lots of us chick crits from Seattle to Los Angeles. In the Bay Area, we ruled.

I was no less than the third woman in a row to helm the *SF Weekly*'s music coverage; at that point, the *Voice* had been around for more than three decades and had never had a female music editor. I took over from Danyel Smith, a lyrical, sensitive writer who went on to become editor in chief of *Vibe* and a novelist. Before Danyel, there was Ann Powers. Ann still wrote a column for us and was working on a Ph.D. She later became a critic for the *New York Times* and then the *Los Angeles Times*. Our colleagues/competitors were *East Bay Express* columnist Gina Arnold, a diehard indie advocate; Lorrie Fleming, a whip-smart blonde holding her own in the muso-land of music magazine *BAM*; and Seana Baruth at the radio trade publication *The Gavin Report*.

I moved to San Francisco with an outstanding assignment for the *Voice*: to find out where all the female rock critics had gone. There used to be many, beginning in the '60s with Ellen Willis at *The New Yorker*. Most had fled the field. In finding them, digging their articles out of microfilm files or following I-know-someone-who-knows-someone-who-knows-someone leads, I discovered a lost legacy. "The Feminine Critique: The Secret History of Women and Rock Journalism," published in the *Village Voice* in the fall of '92, was not just a tribute to buried voices but a declaration of a new generation. The article became the basis for a book, an anthology of these writings edited by Ann and me called *Rock She Wrote: Women Write about Rock, Pop and Rap*. "Now I have female peers, but I never had female role models," as Gina said.

We girls had our own club now.

The women were fierce out West, all Calamity Jane tough. I first saw OGs (Original Grrrls) Bikini Kill in a punk space in Berkeley. Kathleen Hanna, a performance artist with cheerleader moves who performed in a bra with words scrawled in black Magic Marker across her flesh, was riveting. Women were taking off their tops as if they were burkas. I first saw a drummer do it one night, in a completely nonsexual gesture: She was hot; like thousands of male percussionists before her, she shed her shirt. Several members of the all-dyke band Tribe 8 often performed bare chested, like any other hardcore act. I saw them in a little Mission club one night, girls going wild—for themselves, not a camera—in the pit. Singer Lynn Breedlove pulled a strap-on dildo out of her leather pants and got male audience members to suck it. Then, on the song "Frat Boy," she whipped out a knife and hacked off the vinyl appendage. The song offered this lyric solution to a gang rape: "gang castrate."

Something's happening, and you don't know what it is, do you, Mr. Jones.

A couple years after he sent that letter from Cambridge, Brett finally came back to the United States. He had come out, but he stayed away, maybe letting the dust of his confession settle. He flew into New York one summer day. My big brother had left Beloit a short-haired prep, sympathetic to Reagan — that neocon stage was far harder for me to take than his being gay. The brother I met at the airport had a pierced ear and bright, colorful clothes. He was smiling and enthusiastic, a bubbler of talk, stories, and laughter. It was the Brett with a favorite stuffed Scotty dog and the new Clash album, the brother I had known too little for too long.

Brett's bombshell was dynamite blowing up a derelict building. The family absorbed its impact amazingly well. My parents were scarcely surprised, even though it was a subject we had managed never to talk about. Mostly, they were worried about the discrimination Brett might face as an openly gay man. Dad didn't mind Brett's choice of partners; he just didn't understand why he had to advertise it. (He also made the classic statement to me, "Well, it's up to you now to provide the grandkids." That was the wrong thing to say to a rebel girl; I spent the next seventeen years resisting that pressure.)

Dad didn't understand that in the '80s, more than ever, coming out wasn't a choice; it was a necessity. The government's slow response to the way AIDS was decimating the gay community made visibility a matter of survival. As ACT UP put it in their succinct slogan, Silence = Death.

I admired my brother's courage, his refusal to be mute. I wanted to hug, hold, support, and celebrate him. And I was terrified. My brother's sexual identity emerged almost in exact synchronization with the AIDS crisis. I knew Brett was smart enough to practice safe sex, that he hadn't spent the '80s running around in bath houses. But, sometimes, I panicked to think I could lose the wonderful man I had just refound.

Thank Hera, Brett and Paul were lucky: The AIDS epidemic never affected them personally the way it shaped a generation of slightly older gay men. But in the era of ACT UP and Queer Nation, they were, inevitably, galvanized. Brett poured his incredible mind and integrity not into direct-action tactics but into trying to reform the system. In the post–Harvey Milk era, he was an officer in San Francisco's gay Democratic Alice B. Toklas club and instrumental in several political campaigns. When United Farm Workers cofounder Dolores Huerta had her spleen busted after cops got rowdy at a 1988 demonstration, Brett was right there, crouching by her side until medical help arrived. I put my feet where my mouth had long been too, meeting Brett at gay-rights marches on Washington, with him riding a Greyhound from San Francisco and me on the bus rented by Rocket from Providence. During my year in San Francisco, we went to pride marches and street fairs together, along with concerts and movies. It was funny to see my brother openly eyeing men, even as he held his boyfriend's hand.

Paul was the Alice B. Toklas to Brett's Gertrude Stein: the supportive, communicative, gregarious wife. He could be a princess, too, leaving the dirty work, like driving and building things, to Brett. I'd never thought of my brother as the manly one; it's all about perspective, I suppose. I liked Paul instantly and increasingly. He was my age, liked to talk about books, and played a mean badminton. I suppose that as I often dated men who resembled Brett, Paul was a little like me. He understood my family's passive-aggressive power dynamics and made fun of and navigated awkward situations expertly. When Brett clammed up, Paul would always talk. My parents and I have learned to call him when we really want to know what's going on in their lives.

Paul was and is Brett's first and last real boyfriend. I don't know anyone else our age who has had such a strong, loving, long-lasting relationship. They like to joke that they're straighter than I am: a conventional married couple, holding down good jobs, paying their bills, not interested much in partying or drugs. Brett got multiple degrees, in economics and law, and now teaches at the University of Minnesota. Paul, a native Californian who spent almost four decades of his life without living anywhere snowy and cold, proved his love by following my brother to the upper Midwest, where he's a telecommuting attorney. I'm fiercely proud of Cole's gay uncles—though sometimes I'm a little embarrassed to admit they're both lawyers.

7

Noise Equals Life

❧ ❧ ❧

Shortly after midnight on January 21, 1993, my poet friend Mike, his girlfriend Silver, and I climbed into my pickup and headed to Washington, D.C. Being dyed-in-the-wool New Yorkers, they didn't know how to adjust a rearview mirror, let alone drive, so I was pilot of this freedom ride. My funny friends were amazed by the world of fast-food-filled rest stops, as if they had disembarked from a spaceship into a foreign galaxy. They had become two of my top coconspirators; the Tylers, I called them, even though they weren't married. Silver had fled her new age cult family into Mike's arms a decade earlier, leaving her real first and last names behind her. It was the start of a time when half my friends lived under colorful pseudonyms: Magenta, Tinuviel, Victoria, Jana. Silver was a musician, a rock 'n' roll Emily Dickinson who wrote songs in her home studio but never played out. A couple months earlier, I had stayed at the Tylers' West Village apartment all night, playing records, drinking wine, and watching the presidential election returns come in. Lonesome for Big Red, the

Nuyorican, friends, and lovers—and never quite finding my berth in the more tribal Bay Area—I had just moved back to Manhattan.

Now, we were heading for William Jefferson Clinton's inauguration. We didn't have tickets or anything. We were just fans.

We arrived in the capital during a gray, cold dawn. The streets, which I was used to seeing filled with placard-waving protesters, were eerily empty. We shivered outside the White House gates, waiting for I don't know what. Suddenly, a motorcade rushed by. We couldn't see through the dark windows of the limousines, but we convinced ourselves it had to be Bill (or, at the very least, Al). We huddled with the masses on the National Mall, hearing Maya Angelou read "On the Pulse of Morning." We weren't invited to any parties, not even the ball hosted by MTV. That was okay; the people had the power again.

At the end of that sleepless but momentous day, I turned the Toyota around and headed back to New York. Silver and I kept awake by singing into the light breaking over Manhattan. In our tired, happy voices, the Beatles' "Happiness Is a Warm Gun" sounded like a new-generation hymn.

It's simplistic to hinge an entire era on the leader of one nation. But just as Reagan had driven my family from California and was symbolic of everything that had gone wrong with the world as soon as I became a grown-up, Clinton was from a place called Hope. He brought the White House musical library out of mothballs. That was all I—we—needed. For people like the Tylers and me, who had kept the faith through the three successive Republican terms that had accounted for our entire adult lives, Clinton's election was our Berlin Wall falling.

If the '80s were a decade of excess and escape, the '90s exploded with action. Apathy was out; activism was in. The young people whom MTV's Rock the Vote campaign dragged to the polling booth helped elect a sax player to the country's top office. A million black men marched on Washington. Animal lovers and tree huggers made vegetarianism glamorous and fur ugly. ACT UP and Queer Nation turned the AIDS crisis into a gay-rights Waterloo.

Music found its tongue too. Hip-hop was being pushed and pulled by sometimes contradictory, challenging currents: the progressive strains of the Native Tongues clique and the cowboy thuggery of gangsta rap. Punk *had* finally broken in America (as a Sonic Youth movie put it), although now it was called grunge; its boy wonders wore dresses and smooched on national TV. Youths were forming their own tribes at underground rave parties: Critic Simon Reynolds dubbed them Generation Ecstasy. The new musicians weren't afraid to take stands; they were Niggas with Attitude, Bitches with Problems, as two groups dubbed themselves.

The bitches were leading the pack. Queen Latifah, Monie Love, and Yo-Yo added womanism to conscious hip-hop's agenda; the latter founded the Black Women's Political Caucus. The all-girl L.A. band L7 started Rock for Choice to raise money and awareness for abortion rights. Other Angelena musicians, poets, and artists formed the Bohemian Women's Political Alliance, a sort of League of Women Voters for the tattooed Manic Panic crowd.

These musicians were pushing the overdrive pedals of what was being called feminism's third wave. Authors Barbara Ehrenreich,

Susan Faludi, and Naomi Wolf peeled back the backlash beauty myths that had put the skids on women's liberation in the Republican era. A new generation, inspired by the direct action techniques of ACT UP, took those ideas to the streets. The Guerrilla Girls were culture warriors who hid their identities behind gorilla masks and attacked sexism in the art world with humorous billboards and protests. "Do women have to be naked to get into the Met Museum?" asked a poster in which Ingres's famous reclining female nude from *Odalisque* wore a big, furry monkey head. The Women's Action Coalition (WAC) applied Queer Nation strategies to women's issues like choice and media representation. Their meetings in a New York auditorium drew hundreds.

But the organization that got the most attention was a small group of young punk rock fans on both coasts who had created, through records, fanzines, and sleepovers, an informal network that became known as Riot Grrrl. Shouting "Revolution girl style now!" and "Suck my left one," these women touched all my raw nerves. They reminded me of the musicians who had nursed me through headphone intensive care for years: Patti Smith, Deborah Harry, Joan Jett, X-Ray Spex, Chrissie Hynde, the Go-Go's, Exene Cervenka, Throwing Muses. Only those rock 'n' roll heroines had tended to avoid the f-word like the plague. Some just didn't like its semantics: feminist was too close to feminine, and they weren't the delicate type. Others didn't want to be pinned down to any political stand; they preferred to be lone rangers. Then there were those who had swallowed whole the backlash's misogyny and had a tough time hanging around women. I winced at some of the Neanderthal things my heroines said, like Chrissie Hynde's telling women to shave their legs. One step forward, two steps back.

Riot Grrrls had none of those inhibitions. Many of them daughters of second-wave feminists, they were happy to raid Mom's garrison, brandish her weapons, and call themselves feminists. Concerts were like rallies, where men were sent to the back of the room. Meetings resembled '70s consciousness-raising sessions: Someone would bring up a problem (lack of rehearsal space for bands), everyone would say "amen," solutions would be offered (find a place that could become a communal rehearsal area for women), and actions would be planned and taken (a committee formed to search for real estate).

Through DIY ditties and self-help fanzines, Riot Grrrls urged not just a reclamation, but a retooling, of women's lib. Their goals—equal rights for women—were the same as their mothers', but their methods differed. They were punks, not folkies, anarchists, not hippies. Revolution Girl Style was about taking over the means of cultural production—bands, films, publications, advertising—and remaking them in our own images. It was also about making feminism a youth movement again.

Riot Grrrl was our Velvet Revolution. Silver and I pored over Bikini Kill and Girl Germs fanzines, with their typewritten confessionals and agit-pop artwork. We listened to Bratmobile and Mecca Normal records and shouted, "Get out of my way or I might shove" with L7. We felt like the starving scouts who had finally found their frontier party again. On paper, at least.

There were Riot Grrrl meetings in New York. Silver and I faced three problems as we debated whether to attend. One: Incensed by what they saw as insensitive coverage, Riot Grrrls had declared a media ban, and though I felt like one of them, I was also one of us. Two: At the tender age of twenty-eight, Silver and I were old for

Riot Grrrls. Once again, we were in-betweeners—not yuppies, not quite generation X. What were wannabe grrrls to do?

Our third problem was our own existential crisis: We hesitated not because we had a problem with the f-word but because we weren't the organizational types. Silver was a lone wolf whose cult upbringing had given her a severe allergy to groups. For me, feminism was as valid a part of the commonsense progressive McDonnell agenda as rights for minorities, but if there were Redstockings cells in Beloit, I didn't know about them. In college, I went to one meeting at the Sarah Doyle Women's Center. As with everything at Brown, I felt out of place. They made decisions according to this political doctrine called consensus, which meant that everyone, sometimes thirty or more people, had to agree, or at least agree not to disagree. I didn't see why we couldn't just be democratic and let the majority rule. Wasn't the right to think and speak as we chose the essence of feminism? I refused to swallow my dissent.

My first years in New York, I volunteered with the National Abortion Rights Action League, handing out flyers and caucusing politicians in Albany. I marched in pro-choice rallies in Washington, D.C., and New York. But I never had anyone to talk to on the bus rides. I always felt like my love of boy rockers made me suspect, too "male identified." I couldn't bear "womyn's music," that righteous new age folk shit. I supported the fight for women's rights. I just couldn't stand to hang out with the battalion.

So I gave up on organizations (to organizations' immense relief) and became a one-woman army, invading clubs in combat boots and studded armbands. As an often solitary woman in the front row and backstage, not a girlfriend of the band or a groupie but a working peer, I experienced first-hand the need for feminism. I wrote about women's issues when I could (pre–Riot Grrrl, it was not a popular topic among male editors). "The Feminine Critique" was my first major salvo.

Maybe it was the rebukes I suffered after publishing that article that radicalized me. Maybe it was the year I spent researching and talking to women who could have been my role models but had instead been shut down and out. Maybe it was the editor who passed a story idea I had given him on to his male crony . . . again. Maybe it was being alone in those rooms of my own, just me and my cats, night after night. Maybe it was Kathleen Hanna shouting, "I must resist this psychic death" over Tobi Vail's drums, Kathi Wilcox's bass, and Billy Boredom's guitar. Probably, it was all of these things and more that sent me to a New School classroom (as if in a nightmare, I was back in college!) filled with girls still in their first flush of musical/political infatuation—angry, enthused, irritating, inspiring.

Silver and I were among the oldest women at that Riot Grrrl NYC meeting, but we weren't alone. Still, even later, after actions, fights, concerts, fallouts, and friendships with the group of dynamic teenagers and twenty-whatevers I first met that night, I would say I was involved with Riot Grrrl, but I never felt comfortable calling myself one. It seemed silly and beside the point. Whatever their age, most of the New York group was like us: They were second-stage partisans who learned about Revolution Girl Style as much through the mainstream media as the underground. Sometimes we weren't sure what we were supposed to do, if our activities were true to the founders' spirit. We got bogged down in matters of procedure, personality conflicts, internal charges of racism, and the numbing therapy-speak of self-help groups. Students, musicians, artists, filmmakers, and poets, we knew we were under the spotlight, and we were both cowed and proud.

Noise equals life. Five years of living happened in one. Shows, discussions, hugs, readings, protests, fanzines, the posting of political handbills, interventions: There was always something to do. Sara Valentine, an earnest New York University student from New Jersey, became the lead organizer of Pussystock, a festival where daughters shouted fuck-you poems at daddies and college students strangled guitars. I loaded my truck full of grrrls and drove to the gay-rights march on Washington. I hung flyers, marched, sold T-shirts, read poems in crowded bars, shouted down ugly hecklers. I talked, listened, took action.

At one Tribe 8 show at ABC No Rio, a tiny, anarchist basement space on the Lower East Side, I watched a group of distaff fans encircle and grab by the throat a guy who was bumming their scene with his hostile slamming. They whisked him out before he knew what had happened — the politics of dancing, yeah!

Those grrrls carried away the '80s and brought me back to a Squeeze concert pogo kiss. I had the adrenaline sense that the world's revolution was finally in sync with my own. Real punk wasn't the aggro testosterock of hard core: It was mutant music for misfits and rebels, for soft boys and strange girls.

These were some of the bravest women I had ever met. Two weeks after picking up a drumstick, a teenager would be playing a show. In front of a room full of strangers, students would read spoken-word pieces about having been date raped, testifying through tears. A newspaper article would piss someone off, and she would plaster downtown with her own succinct retort. Riot Grrrls were virtuosos of snappy replies and slogans: "Support girl love"; "Teen love is real." They were tailor-made for the media they hated.

Sometimes I felt like a spy in the house of teen girl love. I didn't whip out a notebook, report to my editors what went down at meetings, or write about my Riot Grrrl experiences. But I didn't hide what I did for a living either. I was certainly not the only writer there; however, I was scribbling for the *New York Times*; they, for fanzines. Several of the teenagers and college students sought my advice. After all, I had a decade of the shit they were just starting to deal with under my belt. I let them know that it was they who inspired me, with their courage and smarts.

I'm sure my presence could be off-putting, intimidating, annoying. Silver and I waged a constant war with some members of the group, who we felt were spending too much time deconstructing—or just plain destroying—themselves and each other and not enough time taking on The Man. We quickly became the subjects of their interrogations. At one painful meeting, I was accused of being a foreign agent. I stood up for myself stubbornly, then cried all the way home. Even on the island of misfit toys, I was a misfit.

And then there were days like June 27, 1993. Under the hot sun, a posse of young women caked with cooling mud strode down Fifth Avenue. Riot Grrrl NYC had organized a float for the annual gay-pride parade. A tall, Go-Go's-loving drummer named Jill drove her brother's pickup truck in from New Jersey—redneck transit hijacked for a day. We loaded a drum kit, amps, and guitars into the flatbed and stuck a pirate flag on the antenna. Rolling between colossi of commerce, culture, and God—the Empire State Building, Rockefeller Center, St. John's Cathedral,

Saks Fifth Avenue—drummer girls, ax swingers, and banshee/sirens made an ungodly racket. The rest of us danced and chanted down Manhattan's spine. In homage to the classic photo of founding punk mothers the Slits on their '79 album *Cut*, we took off our shirts and covered ourselves in wet dirt. We reclaimed epithets—"fat," "slut," "dyke"—by scrawling them in black marker on our bodies. Across my stomach, I wrote "Media Whore." Top-free (as we called ourselves, not topless as in strippers) and ecstatic, like Amazonian war-sheroes returning from battle, we took Manhattan, from Central Park to Washington Square.

Riot Grrrl wasn't the only game in town. Silver and I went to WAC meetings, until wackos—extremists so crackpot they must have been FBI plants—started to take over. So, we decided to get our own party started. I had been meeting more and more women who were impressed with Revolution Girl Style but felt ten years too old to be grrrls. A handful of us started our own organization, Strong Women in Music. We were journalists, publicists, marketers, business owners, and record executives who had worked our way into the industry but were not accommodationists. We spent a fair amount of time griping and bonding. We also made styling T-shirts urging "Sink or SWIM" and organized panels and concerts, including one killer show featuring Luscious Jackson, ESG, and Fifth Column.

If among the grrrls I was mainstream, in SWIM, I was a Bolshevik. I took charge of our "girlie actions," protests ACT UP style. The name came from a line in the Rolling Stones' "Satisfaction," which I saw British blues-punk diva PJ Harvey intone with her big, elastic mouth in a tiny East Village coffeehouse one blessed night, queering Mick's lyric. (Later, a couple SWIMmers borrowed the name for the powerhouse publicity and marketing company they decided to form.) When the Grammys dropped the female rock performance category one year, we promptly organized a protest outside Radio City Music Hall. MTV News's Kurt Loder read my press release almost verbatim on the air, and Sonic Youth's Kim Gordon—on crutches, no less—was among the rockers who came to register their dissent. The Grammys never made that mistake again.

I hosted events I called all-girl listening parties: book clubs for music lovers. Every woman brought a song, explained why it was important to her, then played it. Afterwards, we made a mix tape with annotated liner notes for all the participants. It was a way of sharing, personalizing, and politicizing matters of choice and taste—of making music ours, not the domain of critics and musos with their big-willie authority based on record-collection size and knowledge of vintage distortion pedals.

We didn't listen to records just by women, but their voices carried. It was the latest manifestation of cyclical media interest in "women in rock"—yes, a hyped moment, but also a time when females were genuinely making great records and getting airplay and ink they hadn't gotten for years: Liz Phair, the Pretenders, Missy Elliott, the Breeders, Salt 'N' Pepa, Belly, Sleater-Kinney, Tori Amos, Joan Jett, En Vogue. Once the "Feminine Critique" backlash died down, I reaped the benefits of this passing phase.

I flew to London and drove a car to rural England to interview Polly Jean Harvey for an *Option* cover story. Her debut album, *Dry*, had come out of nowhere (well, Yeovil, England) with its declaration of disdain. Stretching her voluptuous mouth wide,

Harvey wailed like an oracle from the front lines of the sex wars, a farm girl wooed and walloped by the evil city, a diva betrayed by her mortal lover, and a hippie chick who had fallen for bad boy Nick Cave. Boys, culture, indie rock, "you leave me dry," she bemoaned. To all the women who have ever loved their bodies, she crowed, "Look at these, my child-bearing hips" in the goddess-worshipping "Sheela Na Gig." The girl-rock revolution hadn't really started, and Polly was far off in her own left field—like most of the rest of us. Now we had someone to dance with out there.

She and I met at an ancient stone café in a seaside town. Her third album, a blues-heavy opus with songs like mythic legends, was about to come out. She was guarded and stoic, despite the distance I'd traveled—until the tape stopped, and she got all girlie: Was I married? Did I have kids? Did I want kids? In fact, I was in love with the writer who was soon to become my first husband, and visions of family were indeed dancing in my head.

And then there was "The Return of Patti Smith." In '95, after the death of her husband, Fred Sonic Smith, the heroine of my adolescence emerged from the suburban Detroit neomedieval turret in which she had sat out most of the '80s, making babies. I drove to Toronto to catch one of her first shows. Like a vision, she danced barefoot across the stage, an icon incarnate, so ecstatic and drenched with sweat, it looked like she had wet herself. A month later, she was scheduled to read at Central Park's Summerstage, that glorious free podium. I had already had mediated contact with Smith because we included a piece of hers in *Rock She Wrote*. I got back in touch with "her people" (weren't we all Patti's people?) and asked for an interview. One day, I picked up the phone in Big Red to hear a small, husky voice almost like a little girl's: "Hi, this is Patti Smith."

A few days later, I stopped by the East Village recording studio where she was rehearsing. I was the first national journalist to talk to her since her reemergence/resurrection. She greeted me, both friendly and commanding in her wall-eyed stare. Patti wore a white poet's blouse through which I could see she still wore no bra, though having two kids had enlarged and lengthened the breasts I knew so well from that *Easter* poster on my teenage wall. Even more compelling, strangely handsome, and off-putting in person, she could never have been everything I imagined she was, back when I needed someone like her so badly, though she was much more than that too: an actual person. (That article became my first and only *Voice* cover story.)

When I was a kid obsessed with records, I imagined that their makers lived in a world bigger, richer, smarter, and more beautiful than the one I felt stuck in: the world of their imaginations. If only I could meet them, I thought as I sang their songs over and over, maybe some of their fairy dust would fall off onto me, and I, too, could be transported out of the run of the mill.

By my thirties, I was meeting almost every one of the artists whose music was then carrying me away. Some looked up to me, amazingly; some looked down. I discovered that when you meet your inspirations, you run the risk of never hearing their music the same way again. Nothing can destroy a cultural crush like a vapid, haughty, shallow star in the all-too-imperfect flesh.

On the other hand, familiarity can breed respect. You don't need to know any more about an artist than what his or her art tells you, and that's all the press-shy J. D. Salingers, Bob Dylans, and Riot Grrrls of the world want you to know—I respect that. But I've found that there ain't nothing like the real thing. A human encounter can reveal that a hero walks it like she talks it, and then some.

My tomboy soul had never spent so much time with so many women. "Support Girl Love" was one of those succinct surf-sticker Riot Grrrl slogans that captured in three words things I'd been waiting a lifetime to say. I had always prized my female friendships; they were more valuable, and certainly longer lasting, than my romances with men. As future fans of *Sex and the City* would affirm, New York women are not merely independent, strong, sexy, smart, and neurotic shopaholics: They take care of each other. They stand in for the families that have been left behind or haven't been built yet. Plus, they don't expect you to pick up their dirty clothes, or your own.

I had not one, but two, incredible support teams. Jana and Vivien were sister writers, musicheads, and sex lovers; they had the added bohemian credential of being talented musicians. Vivien was a big-busted, red-headed Brit who in the '70s and '80s had covered punk, reggae, hip-hop, and Afro-beat for the London music tabloids. She lived the life I had read about as a teenager in magazines: Johnny Lydon produced her first single; Chrissie Hynde roomed in her flat. Jana was a tomboy bassist who was writing a semiautobiographical account of a dominatrix in Miami. She and I would check out the action together at Fraggle Rock, a glam-punk night for girly boys and mannish girls.

When a man broke my heart, Kathy, Viv, and Jana threw a party to help erase the rogue from my life. We tossed out furniture, painted the walls to resemble a birch forest, purged bad mojo with burning sage, played loud music, smoked pot, and drank wine. We started meeting every couple weeks to share our nascent novels, dubbing our writing group the Fictionaires.

Like Carrie Bradshaw and company, my other posse was a fab four, only we were downtown, not uptown, girls—gay, bi, and straight; black, white, and Asian. Vickie was a DJ, journalist, and kick-butt entrepreneur who had two gorgeous kids with her partner, Linda. Cathay was a former drag king and gay activist who was transforming herself into a lovely pursuer of men and book deals. Dina was a fast-talking businesswoman who had recently moved from Miami. We'd meet for dinner and cocktails at whatever was the hippest—without being chichi—new establishment, then hit the clubs. On Sundays, we did the afternoon worship service at Body and Soul, shimmying alongside the bare-chested Chelsea boys and disco divas.

We were all engaged in a common struggle, one larger than us, being fought by chicks around the world. We were trying to figure out how to be adults as one millennium came to a close and a new one dawned. We were happy inheritors of the gains of '60s and '70s feminism. I don't think any of us liked the term postfeminist; we knew the fight wasn't over, that equality was far from achieved.

But there were aspects of our moms' movement that didn't work for us at all. For instance, some of us liked porn. There were those who preferred lesbian erotica, straight girls who were turned on by gay fuck films, others who were trying to find or make films structured around female desire. We were "pro-sex feminists," even pro-un-P.C.-sex feminists. "I just want to manipulate my girlfriend/I just want to make her scream and yell," Lynn Breedlove sang in a Tribe 8 ode to S&M. If a guy had written those words, we'd have protested, but in Lynn's mouth, they were hot.

We liked to dress up as well as dress down, to create outfits that mixed and matched style signifiers, that teased and fucked them: fishnets under ripped blue jeans, '50s housewife frocks and Converse high-tops, miniskirts and engineers' boots, a boy-beater tank top and low-riding cargo pants. Fetishwear might have been part of our apparel arsenal, but most likely we'd be flaunting it like dominatrices (a high-paying gig at least one of us had in fact tried her hand at). Acting like submissives was a trick, not a strategy; if we were "femme in the streets," we were "butch in the sheets," as Tribe 8 sang. No one would have been likely to call us female chauvinist pigs: That cooptation of our transgressions into boy-toy play came later.

We were a feisty, freaky lot, we '90s feminists, adamant about our careers, desires, and independence, but sometimes full of contradictions. Mostly, we were fighting for our freedom and our identities. Some of our battles were taking place in gender frontiers that seemed marginal to most women's daily lives. I'm not saying my march down Fifth Avenue helped some single, unemployed mother feed her five kids (though I was definitely supporting her right to breast-feed in public). But if we couldn't be who we wanted to on the margins or striding down New York's continental divide, then where could we?

8

Love Will Tear Us Apart

☙ ☙ ☙

Most brides walk down the aisle to a song about sex by the favored composer of the Third Reich. Richard Wagner wrote the "Bridal Chorus"—a.k.a., "Here Comes the Bride"—for his opera *Lohengrin* in 1848 (the same year Henri Murger penned his foundational alternative-lifestyle text, *Scènes de la vie de bohème*). In *Lohengrin*, the familiar processional strains play as the groom brings his newlywed to their honeymoon suite, which is subtly taken up by a giant bed. In general, Wagner had questionable opinions of women and appalling ones of Jews. Outside of its heavy wedding rotation, his music has gotten most play as the accompaniment to Nazi spectacles.

The English postpunk band Joy Division wrote the song "Ceremony" sometime late in their career. An unfinished version of it appears on the odds-and-ends collection *Still*, released after singer Ian Curtis hung himself in 1980 and the band regrouped as New Order. "Ceremony" was the A side of New Order's first single. With and without Curtis's somber baritone, it's a gorgeous, sad, enigmatic tune about miscues and last pleas for understanding, about watching love grow. Curtis, a tormented epileptic, sang with uncharacteristic optimism in a breaking voice. Like Wagner, Joy Division and New Order have been linked to fascism (Joy Division was the Nazi term for war brothels). "Ceremony" is a song of endings and beginnings.

One August day in 1995, I marched onto the big porch of a house in northern Michigan playing the "Bridal Chorus" on my electric Silvertone guitar and wearing a vintage '20s wedding dress and a gorilla mask. After a few obligatory verses of Wagner, my amateur picking shifted into that beautiful, sad swan song with its chiming fifths. Brett was probably the only one there who recognized the melody and got the joke: that as untraditional as this anarchofeminist wedding was, it was still a "Ceremony."

The head-rush that launched the '90s was slipping into a cocaine-psychosis crash by mid-decade. Newt Gingrich and his minions were fucking with Bill (never mind whom Bill was fucking). Grunge had turned into scrunge, a.k.a. punk lite. Revolution Girl Style was curdling into Spice Girl Power. And far from bringing the noise, our cultural idols were going down in blazes of unglory.

In '93 I interviewed Kurt Cobain while he was "producing" a record for San Francisco sludge rockers the Melvins. The Nirvana bard's job seemed to consist primarily of nodding out with band members in the studio lounge. I had issues with Kurt's nihilism (even while accepting it as a stance) and tendency to abdicate personal responsibility. Still, he was a working-class hero, a Riot Grrrl lover, the first pop poet to say "fuck you" to the '60s and the '80s.

For about ten minutes, Kurt—birdlike and unshaven—unfolded from his fetal position and snapped into focus. His blue quartz eyes penetrated mine, as if trying to determine whether I was another parasite or "one of us." For a moment, I feared he was going to throw me out of the studio. He had a right to be pissed; the Melvins' publicist had neglected to tell the media-sickened icon I would be there.

I must have said the right things. Empathy can be an affliction; Kurt was suddenly gentle with interest in my opinion of notorious pig-fucker producer Steve Albini, who was about to record Nirvana's next CD. (Not that Kurt took my advice: to find someone not quite such a knee-jerk jerk.) He talked avidly about how much the Melvins music had meant to him, back when he was a homeless teenage punk in Aberdeen, Washington: "There's so much emotion in Buzz's songs. So much passion and anger." Then his eyes drifted closed, and Kurt Cobain shut down.

A little more than a year later, he shot himself in his Seattle home. My friends and I argued about whether Kurt was a coward or a hero, whether his final punk act negated all he had accomplished or completed it.

Drugs took down the '60s' icons. Guns took ours. Tupac was a rising star of the Bay Area, a warrior, a griot. I thought he was going to lead hip-hop to the promised land—not to thug heaven. By the time Biggie went down, I had assassination fascination overkill. I was disillusioned with the music industry, with stars. My friends were my heroes. I wanted to hold them closer than ever.

Tad and I met during my last days in San Francisco. I felt like I had known him for years, ever since my old beau Brian lived out West and began talking about his intellectual drummer friend. The night Tad and Brian gave me a tour of San Francisco as they knew and drank it, I couldn't help but feel this gangling aesthete's tall, dark, and handsome intensity. He was both nervous and gentle, friendly and skittish, a charismatic push-and-puller. Did I mention he was a drummer?

I didn't see Tad again until several months later, at a dinner party in New York, where we were had both set up shop. The Tylers were there too. Tad seemed intrigued by our little literary clique. A few weeks later, he showed up to hear me read at the Poetry Project. After I ranted alongside three other women rock critics about our almost-famous lives, we swooped down to the Nuyorican with the Tylers. In the wee hours of the morning, this charming man walked me back to Big Red. We hung out on the stoop and compared thoughts on Walt Whitman, Abbey Lincoln, sushi, and love, until, finally, I invited Tad up.

The next day he wrote me a poem: "Always sweet, never sour," it began. That was how I had described my eating habits and how Tad, unlike others, unlike myself, saw me.

Tad connected parts of me: Brian, California, literature, punk rock, politics. He had already written one novel, an abstruse but original romance based on Dante and set in Italy, where he had lived for a couple years. He was just starting New York University's Ph.D. program in comparative literature, focusing on medieval Italy. Unlike the academics I was used to, Tad was in love with writing, not criticism. His brain was full of snippets of literature from multiple centuries and countries. Tad was a soft boy—brainy, romantic, sensitive, an aesthete—but not squishy. He loved baseball and knew how to swing a hammer well enough to put bookshelves up when he moved into Big Red. His seemingly frail, bony body had an inner strength when pushed. Survivor's instinct—the protective reflexes of a kid whose mom once poured hot coffee on him, he said—girded him. Ultimately, Tad lacked the courage of his convictions; that was his—our—tragic flaw.

Tad seduced me with words. He spoke passionately about deep beliefs and high ideals. Love was his religion, and I was a willing acolyte. In a world of equivocators, he made grand pledges of allegiance: "I believe people shouldn't be alone."

That charismatic fervor masked chasmic insecurities that could prompt bipolar-opposite statements about the inevitability of isolation: "No one ever really knows another man's mind and heart." Maybe it was Tad's fear of, or obsession with, solitude that drove him through an epic, uninterrupted, frequently overlapping sequence of romances, as though he couldn't stand to be with himself. He was the Casanova king of serial monogamists—except sometimes, he failed at the monogamy part.

Tad inspired me. I hope we inspired each other. I gave him entrée to my New York world of clubs, meetings, and readings. He turned me on to classic books and jazz singers. We collected Nina Simone vinyl at flea markets, played pickup softball in Central Park, lay in the grass in Brooklyn's Prospect Park and scribbled love poems in our notebooks. I wrote more verse when I was with Tad than at any time in my life. Our intensifying infatuation seemed to demand it.

At night we'd snuggle up to old screwball comedies: black-and-white films directed by Howard Hawks, Preston Sturges, and Frank Capra. Cary Grant, Katherine Hepburn, James Stewart, Jean Allen, William Powell, Myrna Loy, and the rest of that celluloid meritocracy would drink cocktails in glamorous gowns, get stuck in haystacks, or bang on typewriters in newsrooms. The dialogue was always witty; the pratfalls, like ballet. Usually, these comedies ended with class pretensions overthrown, the genders equalized, and the heroes married. I remembered how Mama sat in our Beloit living room and watched *It's a Wonderful Life* every Christmas. I wish I had bonded with my teary-eyed grandmother back then, that I had paid more attention to Capra's optimistic vision of a country where the little guy matters more than the big one.

"Moon River," the Henry Mancini theme from *Breakfast at Tiffany's*, became our song. Tad and I were having that kind of screwball New York romance, full of parties populated by odd characters in tiny apartments. One of his fellow graduate students found a vintage decanter at a flea market and figured out how to make absinthe. Tad despised drugs but saw this as more a literary than a narcotic act, so in a Brooklyn brownstone, we all got stupid.

My relationship with Tad had dramatic flare-ups. As passionately as we'd weld together, we would rip apart. Most of the fallouts were caused by one of us getting jealous, usually of someone from the past. We both had rather illustrious histories, which we bragged about a little too much. I don't know if we were testing or warning each other, boasting or threatening. Tad talked so often about Sacajewa, his Native American ex who could pee standing up, that I fell a little in love with her. We had our first "scene" after I casually, callously referred to some sexual act of my past. Tad shut himself up in his apartment with a bottle of scotch for days. I had to bust into his bedroom, smash the glass in his hand, and dump him in a bath to snap him out of it.

Despite, or because of, the fireworks, I thought maybe I had finally found The One. Tad seemed like a New Man to match my

New Woman act. A professed anarchist and fan of the coed English agit-punk group Crass, he found my punk rock feminism a turn-on and loved Tribe 8 and Mecca Normal as much as I did. He didn't seem intimidated by my career and independence; he had his own obsession—with a romance country, language, and literature. Romancing the romantic, I fell in love with a lover in love with love.

Our second summer together found us in my lifelong summer-vacation land, the bucolic woods of Upper Peninsula Michigan. Alone on a bridge overlooking a creek, Tad and I watched dragonflies mate: hover and join, hover and join. I asked him if he had been serious the day before, when he had grabbed me in a parking lot, tickled my sides, and whispered in my ear, "We should get married."

"Evelyn McDonnell, are you proposing to me?"

"Yes, I am."

"Yes."

Romance always trumps reason in my life. I'm scarcely alone: The get-married directive is engrained into little girls at a young age in such a myriad of ways, even a feminist matriarch can be hard put to screen them out. The wedding medley was my last public performance; my first was a fifth-grade rendition of the schmaltzy chestnut "Turn Around": "Turn around and you're a young girl/Going out of the door/Turn around and you're a young wife/With babes of your own." Even as a ten-year-old wannabe pop star, I bought into the breeder imperative.

Alongside fantasies of being a rock star, traveling the world, writing the Great Novel, having a pet cougar, and driving to the beach in my convertible, I dreamed of the day I would get married. (It would only happen once, I presumed.) By the ocean, on a mountaintop, or in a forest glen. In a fringed leather pantsuit, a beaded flapper dress, or a mod miniskirt. With a punk band, a lesbian Unitarian minister, a poet's benediction. I was already picking out songs for the DJ to play at the reception by the time I was in college (Nick Lowe's "I Remember the Bride When She Used to Rock 'n' Roll," Marvin Gaye's "Sexual Healing"). I mean, I've always loved a good party.

And yet, Tad and I didn't want to follow in our parents' footsteps blithely and endorse a heterosexist, patriarchal, government institution (as shrill voices railed in lefty fanzines). Our serious philosophical, political, practical, and aesthetic doubts about the whole enterprise pulled mightily against our euphoric desire to shout our love from the mountaintop. After all, given how our generation has grown up bombarded with statistical and experiential evidence of the demise of the nuclear family, our peer group can scarcely be blamed for holding marriage at arm's length. Tad's still-wedded parents were an anomaly among our friends' families. Nonetheless, he had a deep anger against his mother (which I think affected all his relationships with women). As for me, my parents' divorce wounds were still painfully fresh (and would make the wedding toasts—during which my dad professed his love for both his wives—an excruciating embarrassment).

And then there were the political arguments. Tad and I were appalled by the way reactionaries were turning this supposedly "sacred" institution into a football that they kicked away from our best friends—our brothers, ourselves. I debated whether I should avail myself of a privilege denied to Brett and Paul, but appeased myself by remembering that I had supported their San Francisco ceremony. I certainly wasn't buying into any vestigial sexist notion that marriage made me the property of my husband.

We wanted to uphold our anarchofeminist views, yet still pledge love and fidelity. Taking our cues (or perhaps appropriating them) from gay couples, we decided to create our own commitment ceremony: no preachers or diamond rings, but testimonials from friends and family and beautiful bands handcrafted from pink gold and agates.

Tad and I approached our wedding as we hoped to live our lives together, as a collaborative work of art. We started with the invites. Cutting words and images from bridal magazines and pasting them into collages, we handmade the cover of every card: bouquets floated surreally over Las Vegas casinos and lace veils; brides puzzled over deep issues like, "Milk or sugar first?" The text inside was made out of cut-up letters, as in a ransom note or the cover of *Never Mind the Bollocks, Here's the Sex Pistols.*

The mask started as a joke. As the wedding day neared, a mounting chorus of previously sane people bombarded me with silly questions: What I was going to wear? How I was going to fix my hair? Did I want a pedicure, a manicure, a facial, a lobotomy? People seemed to assume that because I had decided to get married, I was throwing all my tomboy, punk beauty standards out the window. So much attention was paid to my appearance, and so little to the substance of my changing life, I finally turned to Tad one day and said, "I should just wear a gorilla mask."

Once said, there was no way I couldn't do it. It was the ultimate '90s punk performance art prank, a homage to the Guerrilla Girls.

From the neck down I was an ivory flapper belle; on top I was a beast.

I only remained masked for the five minutes it took for me to pick clumsily—I was barely able to see the strings through the eye slots—through my conceptual medley. Then I took the primate face off and donned a flower crown. Tad looked like Cary Grant in a white vintage tuxedo jacket, on the back of which he had spray-painted the anarchist "A" symbol.

The ceremony was part performance art, part Quaker meeting. Tad and I wrote our own vows, or as we called them, portentously and pretentiously, "The Wedding Manifesto." Like many of our peers, we were trying to reinvent the institution of marriage, to re-deem what was good and boot the bad. For instance, he wasn't go-ing to carry me over the threshold since that tradition is based on the ancient Romans' rape of the Sabines (that was the kind of trivia Tad knew); instead, "I walk through the threshold with one hand through my lover's arm and a can of pepper spray in the other," I jested. There was no priest or civil servant present, "for there is perhaps no figure more odiously opposed to love's beauty than the face of the bureaucrat," I said, sounding a lot like Tad. Besides, if a by-the-books ceremony wasn't good enough for Brett and Paul, it wasn't good enough for us. That sounded like false valor, but my emotional choke-up when I tried to say, "We reject laws and religions that do not sanctify relationships between man and man and woman and woman as equivalent to our own," was real.

"Accept me as your consort in love," we said to each other.

"I do."

Instead of a bouquet, I threw the mask.

There was nothing legally binding about that day. We planned to do our civic duty later at New York's City Hall, like couples did in so many screwballs. We wanted the government formality to be an afterthought to the important event, which was our promise to each other, made cohesive by our community's having paid witness. But somehow we never got around to getting that little piece of paper. I would bring it up; Tad would put it off. That worried me. Like our bass-ackwards proposal, I felt like I was always being put in the lead, when sometimes, I wanted to follow. Was Tad trying to have his cake and eat it too? I had succeeded where the other women had failed—I had brought him to the altar—but I hadn't quite married him.

In deed, that is. In word, we always told people that we were married, that Tad was my husband, and I was his wife.

Tad and I promptly birthed a zine. I had seen firsthand the way the "mediacrity" (as I called the ruling magazine cabal) alternately mocked and exploited grunge, Riot Grrrl, hip-hop's coastal rivalry, and poetry. Increasingly frustrated with the opportunities in aboveground publishing, not just for myself but for many talented writers, I wanted to cross-pollinate my different worlds, to mix Nuyorican poetry and feminist protest. Riot Grrrl's tiny, DIY, xeroxed fanzines inspired us, but we wanted something slightly slicker, with ads, that might even become self-supporting. In a Venn diagram, I pictured our zine as the ellipse where Steve Cannon's multiculti *A Gathering of the Tribes*, the third-wave feminist flagship *Bust*, and the wry, esoteric West Coast *h2so4* overlapped. It was a time, as *h2s04* contributor Dave Eggers has said, when it seemed like a magazine could change the world. It had been almost a decade since I'd published my first zine, *OK Go Now*. In the intervening years, strangely, I had become even more idealistic.

So we brought forth *Resister*. The name combined what Mike Tyler called in one poem "the most beautiful word in the English language" ("resist") with a soul-grrrl salute ("sister!"). We also punned off the electrical device called a resistor, using an old '50s science magazine as design inspiration. The masthead listed me as the "power source." It was my baby, but Tad was at my bedside, and *Resister* wouldn't have been delivered without poet Edwin Torres as our graphic designer. I tapped the talents of some of my favorite artists and writers, who donated their works. Poets Paul Beatty and Tracie Morris wrote about film and TV. We published art, poems, stories, and essays, including early excerpts from Lynn Breedlove's novel *Godspeed*, the first writings on obscure oldies by music historian David Wondrich, an excerpt from Brian's hilarious prom satire *Vomit and Roses*, "The Wedding Manifesto," and a review of Lollapalooza by poet Sparrow. I was cashing in on, and doing, favors for friends. *Resister* created a microcommunity, the resisterhood: artists and intellectuals figuring out how to sell ads, get bar codes, make distributors pay, make the system work for revolution.

We hosted readings/performances/fiestas. At one Meow Mix fundraiser, Margarita La Pussygata performed her cabaret burlesque act, singing Velvet Underground and Leonard Cohen songs in Spanish and removing layers of clothes to reveal skin covered in black filigree tattoos. Jeff Buckley accompanied her on guitar. A year later, the angel-voiced troubadour drowned in the Mississippi.

In addition to our print baby, Tad and I talked about making the flesh kind. We even decided what to name them: Billie and

Dusty, oh-so-clever names that simultaneously alluded to famous female singers and male members of Tad's family.

But our very successes undermined our nest building. Within six months of the wedding, Tad landed a fellowship to study in Florence for a semester. A couple weeks later, I was hired as senior editor at the *Village Voice*, in charge of the paper's influential music coverage. The evolution of the critical canon was being placed in the hands of the woman who had critiqued its sexism: It was a golden opportunity, albeit one freighted with the perils of failure as, even within the office, skeptical male colleagues waited for me to stumble.

The timing of our dual rewards was awkward, but Tad and I knew this was the inevitable fate of academics and their spouses, of dual-career couples in general: being sent to far-off places, hopefully together but often apart. I negotiated a few weeks off in the fall to spend in Italy; we figured our love could weather a couple months apart.

Then, one semester was extended to two. Good for Tad. Not so good for us.

Still, he wasn't leaving until the autumn, and it seemed like we were on an invincible roll. Our bohemian lives got unexpected validation when the *Voice*'s theater editor, a kindly veteran of the weekly named Ross Wetzsteon, who died too young in 1998, asked me to write a feature about a rock opera that had opened practically in Big Red's backyard, at East 4th Street's New York Theatre Workshop. Tad and I were skeptical of the idea of a rock musical about the East Village. I doubted it could be edgy enough; Tad, the Italianist, couldn't imagine someone matching Giacomo

Puccini's emotional intensity in *La Bohème*, the show's model (in turn based on Henri Murger's short stories). The sudden death of the play's creator, Jonathan Larson, was a tragedy that aroused our curiosity. But *Rent* wasn't going to get our sympathy vote.

It didn't need it. We sat in that small theater amazed that someone else saw a value system deeper than tattoos and goatees in the alternative lifestyles we had chosen. Just as *La Bohème* depicted individuals struggling to maintain and assert their humanity as the industrial age reduced them to dispensable cogs, *Rent* is about people's efforts to live and love amid the virtual reality of the information era, about finding "connection in an isolating age," as Larson's characters sing. It was neither show-tuney earnest nor indie-rock hip, or maybe it was a little of both.

Plus, I swear I had a leopard-print coat just like the one heroine Mimi wore.

It didn't hurt that the offstage dimensions of the story were as big as what was onstage. I followed the cast and crew as they bounced from the enormous loss of Larson to the giant high of moving the production to Broadway. Real life was getting more like fiction each day, as the character Mark sang.

Ironically, given its title, *Rent* seemed to bind Tad and me, even as our careers pulled us apart. The musical helped us see our own struggles as bigger than ourselves, as meaningful, political. It also reminded us to live in the moment, to appreciate what we had, rather than going about in our daydream and worry clouds, never landing on earth. *Rent* was propelled by this huge joy for life that Larson apparently had, one that was infectious, precious, and precarious. One that we too easily let slip away.

Barely one year after we'd staked our futures together, Tad left for
Italy. Meanwhile, my job had been giving me levels of security,
power, and privilege I hadn't known before. Not to mention stress.
Within the broad employment spectrum, *Voice* editor is well on
the bohemian side. Still, it's a j-o-b. I found myself running in
place on the New York treadmill at which I had previously scoffed,
competing with other publications, jostling to get ahead. Meanwhile, Tad was immersing himself in illuminated manuscripts. We
were being pulled into distant corners of the world, literally; I
could feel the line between us straining as he packed his books
and clothes.

Still, I thought the strands were tough, that, made of committed
ideals and sealed with guitars, they would hold.

Tad and I talked once a week, but mostly we wrote. My husband crafted great love letters, full of vivid details of daily life in
Florence, creating scenes and characters, making declarations.
Ever the retro romantic, he preferred old-fashioned onion-skin
missives to e-mails. Living in a Renaissance villa, hunkering down
into the life of Dante, he was going backwards in time. Meanwhile, I was burrowing into downtown's burgeoning electronic
scene, checking out the possibilities of the digital future.

We hadn't been apart two months when I visited Tad for a few
weeks in October. It was a chaotic flight: My first plane never left
the ground; at the last minute, I was bumped to another airline. I
had to call our friend Christopher on the in-flight phone to ask
him to get the new info to Tad. I had had trouble reaching my
spouse in the days leading up to my departure; the front desk
never seemed to be able to find him in his room.

Flying into Rome, I let myself fantasize that my lanky lover would be pacing the concourse with a bouquet of flowers, waiting to embrace me. He would whisk me off to our hotel room overlooking a gay, flower-strewn piazza, where we would make love all day.

Instead, as I walked out into the airport, Tad was nowhere in sight. He wasn't waiting outside customs or in the concourse. There was no skinny American novelist in the cafeteria, where I bought a sandwich with mysterious contents and waited, not knowing what else to do, or even how to operate a pay phone. He hadn't gotten my message, I figured. He would call back to the villa eventually, they'd tell him where I was, and he'd find me.

Finally, Tad appeared, nonchalant and *senza fiores*. Yes, he had gotten Chris's message. But he had been out until sunrise with the villa's administrative assistant and missed his bus.

"We sat on the top of a hill watching the light come up over Florence," he said, his face lit with the aesthetic ecstasy I knew so well. "You have to meet Beatrice; she's the most amazing person I've ever known."

"Really?" I answered. "And I thought I was."

Tad stopped for a second and realized what he had said. "Of course, besides you," he apologized. Only then did he wrap his long scarecrow arms around me.

It was a hard first day, getting to know each other again, reloving our eccentricities, wondering what the hell was up with the secretary. Tad had trouble speaking English, he was so unused to it. Even more a chameleon than I, he had become, in his mind, Italian. Me, I was cranky, tired, hungry. In Italy, at siesta time, there's nowhere to get food, I discovered—and grumbled like a spoiled American.

The second and third days weren't easy either. But gradually, eventually, we got the hang of each other. We refound the way our bodies fit together at night, the wooden spoon and the teaspoon. I picked up some words of Italian; he recalled his native tongue. No secretary was going to bogart this dream come true: traveling abroad with the man I loved, two expat writers traipsing cobblestone streets. We dodged Vespas in Rome, tried to keep our feet dry in Venice, drank to Romeo and Juliet in Verona. Then we settled into Tad's room in a villa turned world-war hospital turned hotel turned New York University dorm, on a hill outside the center of Florence.

It was an easy walk downtown (though, coming back up, you wanted to catch a bus). While he was in classes or studying, I strolled the streets and parks of this ancient city. From the Boboli Gardens one day, I watched a rainbow arc across the city and land directly on the golden top of the Duomo. I enjoyed the leisurely Latin lunch, with its pasta intro, main course, *quarto litro* of *vino*, and wake-me-up macchiato. I rambled through shops, museums, and churches buzzing with alcohol and caffeine. I fell in love with hazelnut gelato and handmade Florentine paper, as wildly evocative as a Jackson Pollock painting. I imagined myself coming back to the city and working in a paper shop, learning how to mix the inks and cut the paper to line the insides of notebooks, notebooks that I would fill with the novel I would write.

Or else, I would just wander the grounds of the villa with its olive trees, marble statues, derelict and ancient swimming pool, driveway lined with columns of pines, and stunning views. I had traveled extensively in the United States but had hardly been in Europe. I wasn't used to places so dense with history, so replete with breathtaking

monuments of man-made beauty—places where around every corner and down an alley might stand some centuries-old sculpted testament to love, getting rained on. I'm an Americanist, but Europe
opened my eyes to a pride in artistry and a rejection of fast-food convenience. I loved that the bread didn't taste like Styrofoam, the
cheese, like dust, the wine, like cough syrup. Italian children
weren't packed in bubble wrap so that they wouldn't hurt themselves. They played by the fountains, hung out in restaurants at
night, had eyes unclouded by a cathode-ray glaze. I could see what
Tad loved about the place, could see my love of Tad.

Tad felt it too: us again, together, in a new place.

Italy offered retreat and reunion. We could live in Florence,
Tad said, eke out a poor but pleasant life on his fellowship and my
articles, put out a European version of *Resister*—how hip was that?
I could learn Italian, escape media saturation and deadline pres-
sures, go back to the more self-satisfying (albeit impoverishing)
freelance lifestyle.

In our wedding manifesto, I quoted Rainer Maria Rilke: "and
the great renewal of the world will perhaps consist in this, that
man and maid, free of all false feelings and reluctances, will seek
each other not as opposites, but as brother and sister, as neighbors." Tad and I envisioned our union as one of absolute equals,
partners, collaborators, siblings. But my book, my job, my articles,
and my access to our icons had heretofore thrust me into the fore-
ground. Even before he boarded that plane to Florence, I worried
that Tad was getting jealous of my writing success while neglecting his own studies. Instead of my little triumphs' uplifting him,
they seemed to chafe. Tad wasn't traditionally macho; maybe that
made his feelings of emasculation even more repellent to him.

I was tired of wearing the proverbial pants. I liked the idea of cocooning with my writing and relationship, shutting out the noise of industry hype, letting Tad's work be our main source of income while I drank Chianti and scribbled. I wanted him to show me his world, to learn a new language, a new city, and a new way of being.

The *Voice* gig was a good one, but maybe it was too little, too late. I was no longer satisfied with obsessing about music with other obsessives. I loved working with writers, crafting a section, exposing new acts, and adding my twist to the rock-crit canon. But I was always stressed, perennially behind in my listening and reading and phone calls, sure that the haters were just waiting for me to reveal my weaknesses, then to pounce and disembowel me.

Career or love: the old dilemma. For once, I chose the latter.

Our plan was to move to an allegedly gorgeous apartment atop a building in a square downtown. But in the two months between my visit to Italy and my move there, something went terribly awry. Tad, who had been moody but engaged during our Christmas together in the States, seemed to deflate as soon we landed in Florence. I couldn't get him to talk, to accompany me on my walks around the city, which were now gloomy rather than inspiring, to make love to me while looking in my eyes. I'd quit my job and changed continents for this guy: He at least owed me a good missionary-position fuck.

Instead of setting up shop in the middle of Firenze, we remained stuck in Tad's single room in the villa, like war veterans paralyzed by combat fatigue. He wouldn't explain why we weren't moving, why we weren't talking, why we weren't . . . . I had put

Tad in the position of power in our relationship. He collapsed under its weight.

For some people, sex is the base of their relationship. For us, the lovemaking was good, but it was our belief in each other's work that glued us together. I had always supported my husband's writing; I had published it in *Resister* and passed agents who were interested in my work on to Tad. And he had helped inspire me to explore poetry and fiction, encouraged me to use my imaginative, as well as my analytical, mind. I saw us as Virginia and Leonard Woolf, Lee Krasner and Jackson Pollock—admittedly troubled, but brilliant, icons.

Apparently, my husband felt threatened by my move into his terrain. Cuttingly, one day he told me, "If your novel gets published before mine, I'll kill myself."

Still, I toughed it out, waiting for Tad to thaw, as he had on my last visit. I understood that marriage was about the long haul, that was the point—for better or worse. Impatience has always been one of my worst character flaws. This time, I was going to be patient.

Tad came to me one day and said we had to talk.

"We can't stay in Florence," he said, as we sat on the bed in our little room with its centuries of ghosts.

"Why not?"

"We just can't."

"Are you seeing someone?"

"No."

"It's Beatrice, isn't it?"

"No!"

"What do you want us to do?"

"Go back to New York."

"Together?"

"I'll come back later, when the semester's over."

"You're crazy. What am I supposed to tell people: 'I didn't like Florence, and Tad's okay, he'll be back soon?' After I quit my job?"

"You'll be fine."

"Tad, I won't be fine."

"Okay, I'll come back with you."

"Do you really think we can just go back and pick up where we left off like nothing has happened? Your department will hate you, the *Voice* will hate me. If we can be together in New York, why can't we be together in Florence? If you don't want me here, I don't want you anywhere."

Tad actually seemed surprised by that, like he could have his fantasy life in Italy and keep chewing his bite of the Big Apple too. He was crying now with me; while I begged him to let me stay, he begged me to take him with me, to take him back.

Maybe I should have. Maybe I was being stubborn and cowardly, too. But I wasn't the Tammy Wynette/Hillary Clinton stand-by-your-man kind of woman. I couldn't see how I could just close the chapter on our European life before it had even begun, forgive and forget what had happened, whatever it was, since even as he was ending our relationship, Tad wouldn't say what was wrong.

We dream of the day we get married but not of the one we separate. A line from a Springsteen song went through my head again and again as I flew back to New York, my body wrecked and weak from sobbing, my head heavy on the glass of the airplane window: "Is a dream a lie if it don't come true / or is it something worse?"

My brain wouldn't confirm what my heart knew until a few months later, when Mike visited Tad in Italy. My ex introduced our poet friend to his new girlfriend, the villa's secretary.

Meet the New Man, same as the Old Man.

9

Wild Things

❦   ❦   ❦

Divorce was definitely not a part of my moon-age daydreams. I had never fantasized about having a failed marriage, never pictured myself dividing up the Nina Simone CDs or explaining to everyone I knew why I was back in town already, three weeks after my going-away party. I understood more than ever the immense sense of failure that sucked Mom under when she and Dad split. Tad and I hadn't just gotten married. Our marriage had been a public statement, disseminated in print, about the intransigence of love in the face of planned obsolescence. We were the Anarchist and the Feminist, now playing the most clichéd roles of all time, the Adulterer and the Adulteree.

I was a mess. But I was also free. The script hadn't just been flipped; it had been ripped. Time to freestyle.

The next six months were my *Lost Weekend*. I was a born-again bachelorette looking for adventure or whatever came my way.

My first act of debauchery was to commit and mutilate. In my altered altar state, emotional anguish was the fallback position, the ground zero to which I would inevitably return. I longed to make that pain physical. In my evaporating life, I wanted something real, something solid, something that wouldn't leave.

I found it in the sky.

If you looked up any avenue in my East Village neighborhood, your eye would land on the Chrysler Building ascending out of midtown to pierce the firmament. I loved its glowing, Art Deco hypodermic needle reflecting the celestial temper or lit like a pointed crown. Its backstory made it the finest monument to human ambition, hubris, glory, and tragedy in a city teeming with architectural odysseys: In an intense competition to build the tallest building in the world, architect William Van Alen hid the Chrysler Building's stainless steel tip inside the edifice. Then, in ninety minutes, he unfurled it to the sky—a spectacular erection in a big willie contest. For less than a year, the Chrysler was taller than any other man-made structure. Then, the Empire State Building eclipsed it. Walter Chrysler accused Van Alen of financial improprieties and never paid him; the architect's career never recovered. But surveys have proved that any true New Yorker knows that his is the city's ultimate jewel.

A woman named Emma inked the top of the skyscraper, from the hood-ornament gargoyle eagles through the scalloped tower windows up to the needle tip, into my upper left arm. The seven-inch tattoo shows Van Alen's glistening glory amid clouds bathed in the pink, blue, and yellow light of sunset, or maybe sunrise. It's one big, pastel phallic symbol for a skinny girl arm.

My lost weekend would end, but its scar would transform me. I could leave the city again, but I would carry this symbol of New York, of the best and the worst of times, around the world.

One night, in a purposely retro moment, I was making out to Led Zeppelin with a young, trendy author. Mid tongue lock, I realized that, as a wild divorcee, I had a certain cultural carnal authority—a form of girl power if you will. I'm sure it had been a long time since anyone had thought I was a virgin, but as a formerly married woman, I was sexual knowledge incarnate.

I spent fabulous nights out drinking, dancing, and drugging, drowning myself in discos where men danced with men and rock dives where women slammed with women. My flings included Lewis, a Michael Jordan look-alike carpenter I picked up at the bar across the street, and Paul, a DJ/artist/writer who was the hottest thing going in the downtown art and music scene.

I also decided to finally pursue a longtime desire: women.

The first subject of my clumsy dating attempts was a beautiful woman with thick, brown-black hair with purple highlights, a great, asymmetric face, like a Picasso painting, and good taste in music. Our mutual friend Sivan assured me that Caroline was interested. So I asked her out to dinner.

We ate at an East Village white-trash-chic restaurant where you could pay $8 to make s'mores at your table. Talk came easy as we had common interests: live music, the New York skyline (Caroline worked for an architectural press), foreign travel, and books. We were both children of divorce and had a thing for artsy, sensitive men. She was magnificently concerned and suitably outraged when I told her the story of Tad. The sympathy was worth the cost of the meal, which I picked up, confirming, in my mind at least, that this was a date.

Afterward, we walked slowly back to her place through a balmy East Village night. Styling in silver Barney's sandals that looked more comfortable than they were, I had foolishly dressed to impress, and my feet were paying the price.

We got to Caroline's building, an enviable Fifth Avenue address just off Washington Square, in which her father owned an apartment. The kiss at the door to her building was short but insulin-shock-inducing sweet. Then Caroline said good night and went inside. I limped home.

I was used to men wanting to fuck the first night, an uncomplicated impatience that fit in fine with my lost weekend lack of agenda. My first date with a woman gave me instant appreciation of the male side of courtship. Women are hard to read. If they always put you in the position of lead, how do you know when you're moving too fast? Having stumbled so badly with Tad over similar issues, I was hesitant. But I did want to see if there was more where that kiss came from.

I was horny and impatient; Caroline was cool and serene. In the end, we decided we were best as friends. It was an experimental artist and Bikini Kill fan who plucked my girl-love cherry. We ran into each other one night at Fraggle Rock, a queer-punk party where the all-girl house band played weekly tributes to AC/DC, Led Zeppelin, Cheap Trick, and the like. Edy bought me a drink; we danced; I ditched the male friend I'd come there with. I lived only a few blocks away. This time, when we got inside Big Red, there was no hesitation.

Exploring the curves and cavities of another woman's body, I didn't get the kind of identity epiphany I watched Ellen DeGeneres's character have as we watched her come out on national TV at my friend's lesbian rock club, Meow Mix. My closet door didn't fling open as I came stumbling out, unfolding like a squished accordion.

Clearly, as I twiddled away time with Lewis and Paul, I wasn't a lesbian. Maybe, I was bi. Men still seemed a lot easier than women. I was used to them. Even when they were assholes.

A lot of my friends switched teams around this time. Some made permanent changes, some temporary; some changed from women to men, some went the opposite direction. We weren't exactly experimenting; it was more like exploring. I came up with a term for some of us, the ones who in style and temperament could have been lesbians, if we could only give up dick: bykes. The future and our identities were still fluid. We were still discovering what we could be as women.

Ultimately, I found myself again by getting lost, literally. In the year of my divorce, I left New York a dozen times: St. Kitt's, Iceland, Belize, California. But, mostly, I came back to the place that, in the wake of my parents' divorce, had become home: the Upper Peninsula (UP).

Every summer since I was five, my parents parked our trailer on a wooded lot a stone's throw from the southern shore of Lake Superior in Michigan's UP. We'd wake up to bald eagles flying up the shoreline or loons calling their chicks. We'd spend the day lying on the beach reading books or walking up the shore to the Big Cranberry River, picking semiprecious agates and statuesque driftwood out of the sand. In the bog where the Cranberry pooled behind sand dunes, we'd search for minnows and frogs. When we got back to the trailer, we'd jump into always-cold Superior. I'd hang out on my favorite underwater boulder, trying to dive off its slippery white head, until my feet turned blue. We watched the sun set over the water as we sat inside our overgrown tin can and ate a late dinner, then listened to the waves crash as we lay in bed.

The Upper Peninsula is a foundling. This bony finger into the Great Lakes is geographically connected to Wisconsin but politically, because of a bizarre nineteenth-century land swap in which Ohio (suckers!) got Toledo, it belongs to Michigan. Like a third-world colony or a call girl, the UP has periodically been reaped of its natural resources—fur, timber, copper, iron—then left, ravaged and depleted, to fend for itself. Snow can fall from October until May. Those winter days are shack-happy short. Cosmic payback, the summer passage from dawn-to-dusk is epic. Between the time the sun rises at 6 a.m. and sets after 9 p.m., you can canoe ten miles down a river, read William Gibson's *Neuromancer*, or fall in and out of love. If there's a full moon (so bright you can read by it) or northern lights (undimmed by smog or city lamps), the sky may never actually get dark. No wonder so many Finns have settled in this land of the lost; it's a New World Scandinavia.

Not even tourism has managed to rescue this American Patagonia from decades-long economic doldrums. It's just not resort friendly: The bugs are too thick, the weather, too unpredictable, the drive from Chicago, Minneapolis, and Detroit, just a little too long, the Yoopers (as residents are called), a tad too hillbilly. On a perfect July day, you can look from one end of Lake Superior's curving coastline of tan sand to another and see only a couple of human dots braving the chilly waters. Then, you either lay your head back down on the sand and sigh—or dash to the house before the stable flies turn your back into a shimmering black mass.

Superior is a moody mother. Big, deep, and dangerous as a sea, she can be as smooth as a sheet of glass or wild enough to take down freighters like the *Edmund Fitzgerald*. Many nights we'd sit around bonfires on the beach watching a storm roll in from Canada: The lightning strikes would grow thicker, the thunder, louder, until suddenly the wind hit, sweeping sparks into a cyclone. In the UP's woods and lakes, I've watched an eagle pull a trout from the water twenty feet away, otters play chutes and ladders on the shoreline, and a black bear mother stand on her hind feet, contemplating whether to swipe us out of the path between her and her cubs. Wild things, I think I love you.

The Upper Peninsula was more than just a sylvan training ground in which to ramble and nurse my globetrotting literary superstar fantasies. The friends I saw there every year—summer vacationers from diverse points of the continent, most of them connected in one way or another to Beloit College—became my extended family. I know the four generations of "the lake people" better than many of my own bloodline cousins, aunts, and uncles. We've grown up together, playing naked in the sand; now we watch our children reinvent our driftwood games.

After my parents split and sold the Beloit house, the UP became the place I returned to every year. There was no real there there, just an empty lot with a shared dirt road. We never built, and Mom sold the trailer a few years after the divorce. But as long as I could sit on the shores of Gitchee Gumee and watch the clouds roll over the Porcupine Mountains, I was home.

In August, I rented a UP cabin for a month. It was a homely little place with a saltwater well and a thin mattress on a squeaky spring bed. But it was a short walk to the beach and near all the other lake people's cabins. (Not only were the McDonnells the only couple to divorce; ours was also the only family without a UP domicile.) I worked on my novel, cuddled with God and Elvis, gathered agates. I tried not to think of the dragonflies three summers earlier, of the gorilla mask and interpretive dance the year after, of the ground Tad and I had planned to break that summer to build a cottage on my mom's lot. I tried to make the lake all mine again. Mine, just mine, grown-up me.

Not just in the tourist spots I'd always known, but in the daily sites of local culture, I met this arcadia's version of bohemia: craftspeople, musicians, park rangers, carpenters. Many of them were old hippies who embraced life in the shelter of the Porcupine Mountains as a respite from corrupt civilization. On the back porch of the old house she had turned into an arts and antiques store, a substitute teacher named Jackie hosted summer concerts for area musicians. Other folks had turned the falling-down cabins of a mining town into a historic destination.

Hanging out in the local bars, with their taxidermy decor, and checking out the monster trucks at the county fair, I also saw the flipside of paradise: unemployed miners and gun fanatics eager to blame their problems on anyone but themselves—particularly on people not, ostensibly, like themselves. Homophobia, racism, xenophobia, and sexism weren't below the surface: They were in my face, as obvious as the ethnic homogeneity and limp perms all around.

The UP, I realized, isn't Mayberry. I began to wonder if, with its paper mill and taciturn oddballs, it could be Twin Peaks: a land of American gothic, Northern style. Beneath the scenic vistas lie rotting corpses. There's a shotgun in every house and miles between neighbors. *Anatomy of a Murder*, the potboiler and film noir story of an army lieutenant accused of killing a man who had raped his wife, was based on a real UP incident and filmed there, in a not very distant past. Just outside our little village of Ontonagon, during deer-hunting season one year, a man hid himself in the trees. His wife came out of their house to walk their dogs. He took aim and shot her dead.

From my little rental cabin that summer, I couldn't hear Superior's waves. I could only hear the occasional sound of trucks and trailers speeding by on the highway. Late at night, unable to sleep, I began to worry I had been clinging to a home, a dream, an America that no longer existed, if it ever had.

Three days before I was set to pack my laptop and cats into my rental car and drive back to New York, a man with a thick moustache pulled up to my cabin in a dusty pickup. There were two little girls in the front seat, one blond, one brunette. I had met Bud briefly a week earlier, when I had stopped to visit Mike, the contractor who was going to build a dream cabin for Tad and me, back when I was still dreaming. Bud was one of the carpenters helping Mike slap together logs and fashion door handles out of driftwood.

I stood on the porch of my little rental, drawn outdoors by the sound of wheels on gravel. The burly man with a Frank Zappa soul patch jumped out of the truck and walked towards me with his baseball cap in his hands.

"How's it going?" Bud said.

"Okay. How are you?"

"I'm good. Hey, me and my daughters are heading into town to go fishing at the railroad bridge. We just plan to drown some worms for a couple hours, maybe get something to eat. It's a quiet spot, and I've got an extra pole. Wanna come?"

It was a Friday night in Ontonagon, the start of Labor Day weekend, summer's last hurrah. I looked at the truck. I'd never been on a date with children before; nor did I fish. But it wasn't like I had anything else planned. And Bud was handsome, in a rough-trade kind of way. After months of drag kings and leather fetishists, chemical cocktails and electronic music, this could be the strangest adventure of all.

"Why not?" I said.

The Ontonagon railroad bridge spans a hundred feet of the Ontonagon River, moving slowly twenty feet below toward Lake Superior. Trains carrying materials to and from the paper mill pass by a couple times a day; blowing their loud whistles, they give people fishing, or teens diving, from the bridge plenty of time to move out of the way. It's a quiet place, idyllic even, except for the toxic smell of the creosote that coats the logs of the bridge and can smear black stains on clothes. I'd been coming to the UP for almost three decades, and I had never been on this bridge.

Bud helped me stick a nightcrawler on a hook, looping it a couple times so it wouldn't fall off at first nibble. He taught me how to hold the bail, cast the line, jiggle the bait just above the river's bottom, yank to set the hook if I felt the pull of a fish biting, and then reel in hard. I gave it a few tries. But I kept hooking logs and weeds, not fish. The girls, bored, looked at me as if I were an idiot. I quickly realized I was using their pole.

"Why don't you show me how to do it?" I asked them.

"That's okay," the dark-haired older one, Karlie, said sweetly. "You can do it."

"I'd rather just watch," I said. "Really."

"I'll take it," Kenda, the younger blonde, said. Soon she had caught two fish, and everyone was happier.

"See those houses over there?" Bud pointed to a neighborhood of small family homes on the east side of the river. "I grew up there. We called it Diaperville because there were so many of us kids running around. See the water tower there? That's what brought my dad to Ontonagon. He traveled around, painting water towers, until he saw this place and decided to stay. Then, he worked for the newspaper, operating the printing press, until he burned his feet in lye. Then, he became a cop, a sheriff's deputy. Everyone liked my dad. There were cars parked a mile away from the funeral parlor when he died ten years ago. I had come back from working the oil fields out west after he had a stroke, told the hospital 'okay' when they asked to pull the plug. Then, I decided to stay here, have a family."

Bud was Mark Twain reincarnated, a boundless teller of stories about an America still vitally connected to its frontier days. He had laid pipeline, logged trees, been a weekend warrior testing ordnance for the army and Boeing, and worked underground in the White Pine copper mine before it closed. He was a "real man," not a new man—on the flannel-shirted surface at least. A working-class hero straight out of a Springsteen song, he reminded me of my calloused uncles, of guys I necked with in Beloit. I thought about the urban cowboys I'd met in New York, the pathetic William Burroughs wannabes who'd probably piss their pants the first time they got into a saloon brawl. Bud had saloon-brawl stories galore.

The girls rolled their eyes at tales I'm sure they'd heard a million times, but they also hung on Bud's words; their devotion to their father and awe at his experiences were palpable. They were quiet, eyeing me shyly, warily, until Kenda would confront me directly with her big blue eyes that seemed to dare me to find them innocent or sad. Already, at six and eight, they were long-locked beauties. Karlie had her dad's curly brown hair and striking green eyes that were all her own. Kenda was a Polish ghost, the spitting image of her mom, a local beauty who had lost primary custody of her daughters to personal demons. Aware of their delicacy and defiance, I didn't press them with questions.

The girls and Bud were just catching small bass, no keepers, none of the hulking walleyes about which Bud, of course, had ample fish stories. Night was coming; the mosquitoes were starting to bite.

On our way back to the truck, Kenda and I were in front, making a game of balancing on the railroad ties, when we saw something black and white on the tracks ahead. We both stopped, watched the critter amble off into the brush, then looked at each other, our faces flushed with excitement, our guards dropped for shared love of nature.

"Dad, Dad!" Kenda called. "We saw a skunk."

"Really? Where?"

"We did," I nodded. "Up there."

From Diaperville, we drove around back parts of the UP that I hadn't known existed, past old apple orchards and mostly unused farms, trying to find the girls' mom, with whom they were going to spend the weekend. She wasn't at her mom's, wasn't at her friends' camp; no one knew where she was. The smile went out of Bud's face; the girls lapsed into a studied indifference, staring blankly out the window like they'd been down this road a hundred times before.

So, we all went to Bud's place together. It was a family date.

Bud had my dream house: a wooden cabin on the mouth of a creek feeding into Lake Superior. He had built it himself, with the help of friends who worked mostly on the barter system. Bud's "shack by the pond," as he called it in characteristically home-spun, understated fashion, was rough and unfinished. But it was as moving and accomplished as any of Brian's plays, Jeff's paintings, or Ed's poems. It was better than Tad's novel. Bud felled the red pines of the outer walls himself, planed them, and left their edges uncut, the bark still clinging to them. The ceiling rose into a cathedral point. The front of the cabin pushed into the creek shore like a ship's bow.

You had to walk a log suspended over Pine Creek to get to the beach. It was dark, a moonless night, when we crossed, so Bud held my hand. He kept holding it as he guided me through the trees on the other side. We were still holding hands as we sat on a log looking out over Lake Superior, talking and talking and talking.

I had a hard time believing some of Bud's most rough-and-tumble tales. Then he would show me the physical evidence. Every scar had a story. The missing third of his ring finger: It got caught in equipment out in the oil fields. The line on his shin: While he was working as a lumberjack, a tree fell on him and broke his leg. The circles in his thigh: He shot himself while cleaning a rifle. The slight walleye: He was hit in the face with a board outside a bar while defending a woman's honor. The jagged white mark on his elbow: He broke it arm wrestling.

But he wasn't some roughneck prole; he was more like a north-woods libertine. His soul patch was an homage to Frank Zappa; sushi was his favorite food; his favorite singer was Chrissie Hynde (even if he called her Heinz). An amateur philosopher, many of his stories had a point, like the one about how on their deathbeds, the thing people said they regretted most was not having loved more.

It wasn't just that he was the salt-of-the-earth type; there are plenty of dumb-fuck rednecks in the country. I think being a parent grounded Bud in a way that was novel to me. Bud spoke of his daughters with an impressive wisdom. He said that being a single parent had given him deep empathy for the women who did this all the time.

"How did you know you wanted kids?" I asked.

"I just always wanted them and knew I was ready. I'd been out west, sown my seeds. The only mistake I made was presuming my wife felt the same. Maybe I pushed my readiness on her."

"Isn't it hard?"

"Fuck yeah. But I've learned the most important thing in my life from my daughters: unconditional love."

Unconditional love. It made me want to cry. What did that feel like? I wanted to know.

Bud and I spent the weekend together. The girls were leery of me at first. Then, on Sunday, I showed up with a bag of leftover food that I wouldn't be taking to New York with me. The girls squealed with such delight as they packed cookies, chocolate bars, marshmallows, and Graham crackers into cupboards that I wondered when they had last seen groceries.

"Thank you, Evelyn," Karlie said, and gave me one of the hugs that I would come to know as the best hugs in the world.

"Can she stay the night, Dad?" asked Kenda, who had stubbornly stayed up with Bud and me the night before, watching a movie despite droopy eyes, daring us to try anything physical while she was awake.

"Can she?" Karlie chimed in.

"I guess so," Bud laughed. "That is, if she wants to."

"Well, I suppose I can." I laughed too.

Karlie and Kenda were in the Labor Day town parade the next morning. Bud and I packed my stuff into my car while they were getting ready with their fellow marchers. There was a late-summer heat wave; we were dripping with sweat. Bud washed my hair for me in the shower; his hands massaged my scalp tenderly. Then, he poured cooling saltwater down my back.

"If you ever want a little taste of family life, we'll be right here," Bud told me.

We raced into town to catch sight of the girls and their friends carrying a crude Chinese dragon through the main street of Ontonagon. I winced at the lines that had been drawn in the corners of their eyes to make them look Asian. Then, I waved. I waved all the way out of town, looking back in my rearview mirror at this strange man and his beautiful daughters.

What had I gotten myself into?

"If you ever want a little taste of family life, we'll be right here." Bud's words echoed in my head. Instead of being through with Michigan, I came back in a month. Bud and I spent two weeks of Indian summer that were as close to storybook romance as I've known: long walks in the woods, canoeing, a weekend of jazz and sushi in Madison. Then, we spent two months together. Then, two years passed, the two of us driving back and forth, New York to Michigan, like love-struck kids. For the first time in my life, I saw the UP in all its seasons. Maples, birches, oaks, and poplars turned the Porkies into a calico quilt of gold, red, and brown in the fall. I toasted the new year swaddled in layers of winter wear, standing on Superior icebergs. I watched lady slippers—the girls called them pink butts—unfurl all over Bud's property in the spring. When the lake people came back in the summer, I was able to show them areas of the UP we had never heard of before: Mount Baldy, Prickett reservoir, the tailings dam.

As different from skinny Tad as could be, Bud was definitely rebound material. He was a deer hunter, a mountain man, a true Yooper. It had been a long time since I'd dated someone who didn't have a book or CD collection, who was twice my girth (all muscle), who could pick me up and twirl me around—whom I would let pick me up and twirl me around. Many of my sweethearts over the years could pass for the effete side of gay, or at least metrosexual. In homosexual iconography, Bud was a burly bear.

We had unexpected things in common. Our mothers both came from the poor South. Whereas mine had fled her upbringing, however, Bettie Lou was very much a proud product of hers. Half-Shawnee, Bud's mom married when she was twelve and had three kids by the time she was eighteen, then adopted a fourth. His dad, Gene, had polio when he was a boy, but a slight disability hadn't kept him from becoming a consummate do-it-yourselfer, the man who taught Bud the basics of carpentry, plumbing, and auto repair. Bud's brother fought in Vietnam; afterward, he mostly kept to himself, with his wife and their horses. His older sister, Babette, had trained to be a hair stylist, but the dyes and perms gave her migraines, so she worked as a nurse's aide. His younger sister, Peggy, was an accountant. All three siblings had been divorced once. I could picture Walker Evans photos illustrating Bud's family history as written by John Steinbeck. It reminded me of Mama and her brood.

Bud had boundless intellectual curiosity, an open mind, and a quick intelligence. He had barely heard hip-hop outside of MTV, but Missy Elliott's *Supa Dupa Fly* became a soundtrack for our romance. Or we would listen to Katell Keineg eulogize surrealist Leonor Fini and condemn men's need for conquest in her gorgeous Welsh burr. Women's voices soothed the savage Bud, whereas I leaned toward music that whipped me into a lather.

I saw in this woodsman a soul mate, someone with roots in rich Midwestern soil who kept the free spirit of the '70s alive. Sure, he was rough around the edges. But did I want someone who had a complete set of black ceramic tableware (like Tad) or someone who had living proof of his commitment to family? Cities are supposed to be home to the New Men, but all I was meeting in New York were neat freaks unable to stick to a pick in the boundless urban variety pack. Bud needed a little updating, but his engine was good.

I think what I liked most about him were his daughters. In my New York circle, I didn't know a male mature enough to have kids, let alone raise them on his own. I fell as much for Kenda and Karlie's sweet thank you's and scraped knees as for Bud's bear hugs and mutilated body. They were cool, smart, loving, independent—maybe too independent for their tender age. They had already suffered more than I ever had: their parents' bitter and violent divorce, their mom's drinking, their dad's temper. Their mother left them in a truck that slipped out of gear and rolled into a creek when they were toddlers. Deb later redeemed herself by rescuing Kenda when their house burnt to the ground.

But the girls weren't damaged goods; they exuded sweetness and beauty. Karlie was generous and kind tempered to a fault; Kenda was both a crack-up and stern truth seeker. They were playful and combative with me. One winter day, we hiked through the woods to a cabin in the Porcupine Mountains where Bud's sister was staying with a group of kids. On the way out, the girls started bombarding me with snowballs. I launched a counterattack, and soon we were in a full-blown war, wrestling in white powder. Bud says that when he saw me sitting on the girls, rubbing their faces in the snow, he didn't know whether to admire my country pluck or worry about the future.

Watching Kenda and Karlie romp in the lake, refuse to wear dresses, and dance to *Supa Dupa Fly*, I saw my tomboy self, three decades ago. I'd been looking for causes, for a mission to be part of, my whole life. Well, how about this little family?

10

Kick Out the Jams, Mothers

Oo Oo Oo

There are life paths we seek, and there are surprise detours. You can either get lost on those detours or get found. I don't think anyone ever foresees becoming a stepparent—although, given Western civilization's divorce and remarriage rate, it's a strong possibility for a growing number of us. I had no idea what I was in for when I, a thirty-two-year-old East Village bohemian with virtually no experience with children, hooked up with Bud and the girls. If I had seen the future, with its piles of laundry and bitter rebukes, I might have run the other way. Still a kid myself in many ways, self-centered and hedonistic, I was ill prepared for the hardest task I'd ever taken on. Stepparenting, I was about to discover, requires all the work of parenting, but the rewards are fewer and longer in coming.

Fortunately, when they did come, they were worth every piss-stained, bad-mouthed, self-sacrificing minute.

The impracticalities of our relationship just made Bud and me love each other harder. The biggest hurdle was basic: how to be together. Michigan was romantic—in the short term. But the misgivings I'd had about isolated, small-town life before I met Bud were further validated the more time I spent in the UP, the more I heard offhand comments about blacks, gays, Jews, and Asians that made me feel like I'd stepped through a time tunnel back to a pre–civil rights America.

Bud's friends and family accepted me immediately, tattoos and all. But sometimes, when eyes followed me at the supermarket or I got hostile looks at the bars, I felt like a curiosity, or worse, an evil city woman trying to lure away a native son and a barren sinner trying to take over his daughters. Being unmarried and childless at my advanced age, I was clearly defective in the local view. Bud's sisters, working moms themselves, always showed genuine interest in my career; a Blondie fan, Babette was pleased when I gave her a Deborah Harry biography for which I'd written a foreword. But theirs was not a reading-inclined family. I think his mom thought I was just fooling around all that time I spent sitting at the computer. She couldn't understand why I wouldn't watch the girls while I was writing. I was home, wasn't I? So I couldn't be working.

I had admired Bud's immersion in the wilderness, the way he'd chosen, I thought, to drop out of the electric grid. But I soon realized that he had no phone because he had trouble paying the bill. That was a big problem for a long-distance relationship, so I forked over the cash to get him hooked up.

I'd been so smitten with the natural beauty of his house, I'd overlooked the signs that this little one-provider family was living precariously close to the edge. Bud got his water from a line into Lake Superior—which would freeze during the winter. He also had trouble affording the heating bills. They essentially spent half the year living with his mother, who, I realized, played a giant role in raising the girls.

Bud quit his job with Mike shortly after we met, then struggled to make a living with other contractors and as a logger. His problems weren't just his own: Ever since the copper mine had closed several years earlier, the area had been severely depressed. The tech boom didn't have much impact on this part of the world, beyond bringing fake naked pictures of Britney Spears into backcountry bedrooms.

I wasn't exactly going to find editorial work in a county with only ten thousand people and one eight-page weekly newspaper. Nor was there a great demand in New York publishing for articles about the UP. I did get one great gig for *Travel and Leisure*. I spent a week exploring the ghost towns and art galleries of the Keweenaw Peninsula while Bud cut down its trees. At nights, we'd meet up at old copper-baron mansions and lighthouses turned into bed-and-breakfasts. In the mornings, we'd set off for our divergent occupations: Bud chopping the trees that created the pulp for the paper for the magazine.

After two years in and out of Michigan, it became clear I was not going to be able to stay there; the country life was not for me, darling. Meanwhile Bud had begun making the thousand-mile drive to New York for weeks-long visits. The first time he came, he crossed the George Washington Bridge three times trying to figure out how to get into Manhattan. By the time he pulled up to Big Red, he was spent. "What a fucking nightmare," were his first words as he got out of his Bronco (trying to impress me, he had traded in the pickup), which was still splattered with the mud of Michigan.

He got over it. Bud had lived in cities: Lansing, Memphis, Little Rock. For a Yooper, he was worldly, had spent time in Las Vegas, Park City, and Los Angeles.

Bud's readiness for new experiences was one of the things I liked about him. He had that small-towner, star-struck awe I remembered that I had when I first got to Gotham. He loved being in a place where he could go to the bar across the street and see his favorite actress, Janeane Garofalo, or nod hi to Susan Sarandon on his way to work. Sometimes, the nightlife gave him vertigo. He got short of breath and almost passed out at a couple gigs; he wasn't used to being in small, smoky places with so many people.

Bud took to most of my friends instantly, and they to him. A few thought I was crazy to be with someone so "unrefined," who came with so much cultural and personal baggage, especially when I had so recently been dating hip DJ and novelist bachelors. Others worried about my putting my heart into a difficult situation again, so soon after Tad. They were all right, to a degree. But I had to make my own choices.

Putting up bookshelves, lofts, and cabinets, Bud could make more money in New York City in a couple of weeks than he could make in Michigan in a month. Meanwhile, the girls stayed with his mom, or sometimes with their mom, or their aunts, or Bud's neighbors. They hated the instability and resented the fact their dad would leave them to be with me. It was a difficult, untenable situation for everyone.

I thought I had known hardship before: The two years Bud and I spent traveling back and forth between Michigan and New York were often nightmarish. He had legal troubles that made it difficult for him to move. Karlie and Kenda didn't want to leave the only home they'd known. New York couldn't have been more different from the UP if it were a foreign country. If they didn't want to move, their mom wasn't going to let them, and we couldn't take them out of state without her permission. Bud kept saying it was going to happen, but I began to lose faith. I was sick to death of long-distance relationships. I didn't trust them; I didn't know— didn't want to know—what Bud was doing during the months we were apart. Thank god he didn't have a secretary.

Finally, one late summer day in the last year of the millennium, Bud, Karlie, and Kenda pulled up on East 5th Street in a rusty van full of carpenter's tools. On their laps was a Yorkshire terrier puppy. Mr. Otis was the bribe Bud had resorted to in order to win the girls' consent, without my knowledge. I, in my new role as Mother Hubbard, swayed for a moment at the thought of the life that was about to be squeezed into my shoe: two adults, two kids, two cats, and a dog. Then, I picked Otie up and hugged him. Even if he hadn't turned out to be the coolest, smartest dog on planet rock, he was worth every penny.

Whoever first said, "It takes a village to raise a family," was definitely not talking about the East Village. Otie was a cutie, but the girls were the real exotic pets in my hood. People stared in wonder at their babes-in-the-woods beauty as we lunched on nouvelle Asian cuisine or shopped St. Mark's Place. In the '90s, kids hadn't become the trendy accessory that they are now. One couple in my building had small children, then fled to England. Vickie was my sole close parent friend, but her kids were younger than mine and lived in Brooklyn.

Many people emigrate from the city when they have kids. I imported youths. And I wasn't merely being selfish (though there was that). Ever since college, I'd envied kids raised in New York. They were street and book smart, tough and knowing. They saw cool bands at CBGB's while I was out skipping proms. They *played* in cool bands at CBGB's while Vince was crooning "Natural High." Even if they didn't know how to drive, they had a self-sufficiency, an ability to navigate streets and cultures, that people generally didn't get from small towns and suburbs.

Granted, the Tylers would have been food for the Blair Witch if you had set them in the middle of the woods. But Bud's girls already had that kind of wilderness conquered. Lawns, garages, family rooms, safe neighborhoods, high school football teams: The trappings of suburbia were traps. Field trips to the Met, multicultural classrooms, brain-trust public schools like Stuyvesant and Bronx Science, Big Bird: In the third millennium, I figured, the girls will need worldliness more than woodsiness.

Becoming an instant city parent (just add bottled water) was both harder and easier than I imagined. Everyone warned me that I would have to be a Machiavellian mommy to get the girls into decent schools. But maybe because the East Village was still relatively child free and its schools not yet viciously fought over, I found it easy to walk into Sesame Street. I found a great alternative public grade school with committed teachers, a small, diverse student body, and an active parents' community full of artists, punks, lesbians, and hippies. None of their classmates seemed to come from "traditional families," so at least the girls didn't have to apologize for their own mixed-up home life.

The girls thought everyone was weird as hell. Maybe they were guinea pigs in my idealistic social experiment. But it seemed to me that the Lower East Side School (LESS) was just the transition Kenda and Karlie needed as they moved from a dying rural school district, whose sole advantage was tiny class sizes. I feared they would get lost in the usual sprawling brick jungle of P.S. whatever. LESS was housed in one of those old, giant buildings, but it was an entity unto itself on the top floor: a Deweyan paradise once you climbed four flights of stairs. There wasn't much of a playground, but the school had access to an adjacent community garden. And unlike in Michigan, it had music, art, theater.

LESS was a few blocks from our apartment. Bud and/or I would walk the girls every morning and some afternoons (when they didn't go to afterschool). Otis would come with. We trained him to walk without a leash; "let a dog use his brain and he'll have one," Bud said—that's pretty much his approach to parenting. In the middle of one block, there was a long wheelchair ramp into a building. Otie, on the ramp, and Kenda, on the sidewalk, would race each other most mornings, their feet moving fast, their hair flying behind them. After school, we'd buy Italian ices or stop for pierogis or hot chocolate.

The girls were troopers. It must have been ridiculously hard for them to leave almost everything and everyone they knew and loved behind. As they had learned to do in Michigan, they comforted each other. Even though they had their own rooms for the first time, they still often slept together, giggling—and undoubtedly complaining about me—to each other.

But they also got to develop their own individual interests, social groups, and identities. They each quickly discovered the New York lifesaver I had found: the extraordinary nature and value of female friendships.

Xian's ponytailed, Jewish filmmaker dad lived across the street from us, her Chinese-American poet mom, around the corner. She and Karlie tied a string across East 5th between our apartment windows. They passed notes and other sundry objects back and forth, as if cell phones had not yet been invented. Xian came to Michigan with us two summers and saw the best and worst of middle America. The mosquitoes ate her alive.

Nadia's mom was a special education teacher and former squatter; her African musician dad lived in Mexico. She had done some modeling, played violin, and had a great singing voice and an even better temperament. For one Halloween, Nadia dressed as a ghost, Kenda, as a penguin. In their costumes and coloring, they were a study in black-and-white contrasts and an inseparable team.

Kenda threw herself into the opportunities that were the whole point of being in a city. She studied trumpet, tried her hand (and arms, knees, torso, and toes) at gymnastics, played soccer, helped the woman who watered the trees on our block, and visited old folks at a retirement home with Nadia.

Karlie was more withdrawn—until you put some sticks in her hand. One day we were visiting a friend's recording studio. She sat down at the drums while the rest of us were gabbing and let off two years' worth of steam. The studio producers looked at us amazed.

"Has she had lessons?"

"No," we laughed. "As far as we know, it's the first time she's drummed."

You couldn't meet those girls and not want to help them. Two different people donated old drums to Karlie. One set went back to Michigan: Karlie whaled on it in the back of the van on the thousand-mile drive. The other we kept in the loft that Bud and I rented in Brooklyn as a joint workspace.

As it is for most New Yorkers, real estate was our biggest issue. Living in my apartment was like being in the family trailer again. The girls actually each had their own little rooms, my old office and bedroom. We made clever use of tapestries and lofts to give at least the illusion of privacy and efficiency. We tried to make ourselves feel better about the tight quarters by pointing out that a hundred years ago, a family twice this size might have shared this old tenement. Or we would imagine we were in a boat on a great adventure, which wasn't that far from the truth; the tilt of the floors, which sent us veering into each other when we tried to squeeze by, recalled the pitch of a wave. Still, sometimes I'd look around at the piles of dirty dishes, cat hair, men's clothes, and promotional CDs and think to myself, I went to Brown for this?

Laundry days were epic. Used to having a washer and dryer in their house and being a carpenter and children, Bud and the girls went through a few outfits a day. Once a week, we'd toss all the dirty clothes on the kitchen floor, the only space big enough for such a monstrous pile. We'd tie them up in sheets, then each haul a load to the corner laundry. We'd pray the triple-load machines were free. Bud was good at turning chores into social occasions and adventures. I'd lived there for eight years and never once

talked to the Laundromat manager; José and Bud became bud-
dies. We'd pass the wash and dry cycles buying paper cones filled
with Belgian fries or reading the Sunday *Times*. Hours later, we'd
still be folding clothes on our bed in Big Red.

Bud and I could have tried to find a real apartment—even a
small house—in one of the outer boroughs or New Jersey. But I
couldn't leave 5th Street. I had a rent-controlled apartment in
Manhattan, damn it! I wasn't ready to give up easy walks to clubs
and restaurants, to become a commuter.

So, we rented a loft as a shared workspace. The thousand-
square-foot bare box sat atop a massive industrial brick building in
Dumbo, the Brooklyn neighborhood so named because of its location down under the overpasses for the Manhattan and Brooklyn bridges. The hood was emerging as the latest artists'
community (to be taken over in about two years by yuppies). Our
building was a warren of painter's studios, illegal apartments, and
website porno operations. Our loft was on the top, tenth floor;
stairs in the hall provided roof access. We had windows on three
sides overlooking all five boroughs. I could see the World Trade
Center and the Chrysler Building from my desk, watch commerce pass on the Manhattan Bridge and the East River as I
mused over the best way to describe a guitar lick. We ran a plastic
sheet down the middle of the loft dividing our territories. Bud
built cabinets on one side; I built stories on the other. We'd meet
at noon for lunch and sex.

The loft was scenic but immensely impractical. Sawdust covered my CDs and computers. I couldn't hear the stereo over the
power tools and had to tell Bud to stop hammering every time the

phone rang. The wind whipped through the room chillingly; the elevator worked erratically. It was a cold and desolate building in a neighborhood where women were being mugged by roving packs of youths. For girls used to having the run of a house, woods, and beach, it must have been terrifying.

Still, Dumbo gave us breathing room and, with those vistas, a feeling of infinite space. It was a great place for readings and parties. With our neighbor Jeff, we'd throw down a swath of green indoor/outdoor carpeting on the roof and have barbecues where we'd watch the sun set over Manhattan. In the mornings, we'd have lunch at Papi's, a Dominican greasy spoon that catered to construction workers, slackers, and the nearby projects. Sometimes we'd picnic down on "Dumbo beach," a tumble of boulders on the East River's shores. Dinner was at Superfine, a healthy boutique eatery run by a lesbian couple. Superfine rented its small dining room from Between the Bridges, an old-school bar stickered with decals from iron-workers' unions. It was an uneasy but excellent juxtaposition that, of course, didn't last. Superfine is now a sprawling, hip restaurant; the bar—that vestige of historic Brooklyn—has been replaced by another condo tower.

Every fall, the area's artists threw open their doors for the annual Dumbo open studios. For residents, it was a chance to see what their neighbors were up to, check out what their spaces looked like, and share a beer with strangers. One year, as slumming arts patrons in Prada shoes picked their way through the decrepit building, Karlie hauled her drum kit up to the roof, put out a hat, and let rip. Soon everyone was talking about the amazing little drummer girl in the sky, and Karlie had made bank.

Our bi-borough solution was a stopgap measure, a temporary solution until we saw if (1) we could make it together, and (2) we could make it in New York. After one year, the verdict was still out.

Part of the problem was stepparenting. Raising a family would undoubtedly have been easier if I had started from scratch. Once you've wiped a kid's ass for a few years, you come to peace with the fact you'll spend your life putting up with shit. Cocooned in my punk rock literary world, I was extremely ignorant of the incredible patience, innovation, juggling, endurance, and sheer chutzpah required for parenting. I was entering this drama in media res, with a couple of ready-mades, a pair of loaners. Normal people warm up to child raising by practicing with nieces and nephews, friends' kids, or at least dogs. I had spent my adult years preparing to be a crazy cat woman. Normal parents have nine months of expecting in which to read the "operating instructions," as Anne Lamott so perfectly describes Dr. Spock's child-rearing books. I not only skipped basic training, but I parachuted into battle six years late.

And I was a commander without portfolio: I had the responsibilities and duties of parenting but not the title. The girls would refer to me as "she," the outsider, often with scornful derision. Throughout her first year in New York, Kenda let me know that she wanted to go back to the Midwest to live with her real mom. Usually, the rebuke would come right after I had gone the extra mile to do something special for her, like bought her a six-foot spicy Italian sandwich from Subway, her favorite meal, for her birthday. She would turn and shout, her eyes red and her face hard, "You're not my mother, and you never will be!"

Out of the mouths of babes . . . . The reproach was inarguable and stung horribly. I would always be the not-quite mom. I hadn't birthed the girls, and as long as they felt that was the prerequisite for letting me into their hearts and lives, all I could do was wait. The more I tried to force myself on them, the more they would withdraw.

The rational part of me knew that the girls were behaving as stepchildren often do. It was obvious psychology: They were anxious to be faithful to an absent birth parent and jealous of the attention being paid to an outsider by the present parent. They still, typically, harbored hope that Bud and Deb would get back together. I tried not to take the girls' resentment personally. Even when they hated me the most, it wasn't precisely me they hated. Well, maybe they thought I was weird. I mean, sure, I took them to their first rock concerts and personally introduced them to Queen Latifah one day, but let's face it, I was still a geek.

Stepparenting is a delicate balancing act, and I'm a klutz. Harsh words must roll off your back. You must never expect instant, or even deferred, gratification. Compared to other stories I've heard, of women physically attacked by their partner's children, I had it good.

Bud's mom always tried to console me by telling me it took her years and years to finally appreciate her father's wife. After hearing the story of her eventual epiphany about a hundred times, I realized that Bettie Lou's stepmother was dead before she finally got her props. A martyr.

I, too, was struggling to grow up and integrate my old and new lives. The summer of 1998 found me in New York's gay-pride parade again: not a fish out of water but a fish unsure of which way to swim. Half a decade earlier, I had marched as an ally who was still in practice, if not desire, straight. In the interim, I had officially earned my bi stripes. Yet, in love with a woodsman and his daughters, I was passing for a breeder. Was I in the parade or out of the parade? And if I was in, what was I going to tell my little family: "Bye honeys, see you later: The sirens of lesbianism are calling."

My Michiganders had big hearts but a small town's limited, negative stereotypes of homosexuality. I often had to tell the girls there was nothing wrong with something or someone's being gay, that the word was not an epithet, not a synonym for weak or wrong or immoral or stupid—that they insulted my family, friends, and me when they used it that way. I explained to Bud early on that I was bi (typically, it made him horny), my brother had a boyfriend, and I was all about gay rights. Considering his environment, he took it all with a pretty open mind. Still, I knew that awareness of Melissa Etheridge and Elton John wasn't going to prepare him and his offspring for the shock of a thousands-strong parade of dykes on bikes and fierce tutu-wearing fairies.

In '98, our little posse of freelance queers didn't march under any specific banner. Our official coalitions had come, or were coming, undone. Whereas a few years earlier, taking part in gay pride day was a given in my circles—kind of like going to Lollapalooza—in '98, many of us were MIA. The times were changing, the cultural pendulum swinging back to a period of moral retrenchment, of unfun fundamentalism. I wasn't about to run out on my friends. But this time, I did keep my shirt on.

After all, bless their hearts, Bud and the girls were watching—long enough to lend me their support at least. I felt proud and dopey when we walked by them. Bud clapped. The girls looked confused and embarrassed. Then, we were past.

At the parade's end, my friends and I milled about Washington Square, trying to decide what to do next. There were parties all night, hookups in bars. Edy was there, part of the circle of friends, snapping pictures. It felt good to hold her hand again, a comforting gesture reminding me that it—girl love—hadn't all been a dream. We talked about my/our struggle, change, the craziness of life. I think I was rambling, trying to make sense of the inchoate, to fix what wasn't broken, just unformed.

Edy stopped me with a word of advice, sealed with a goodbye kiss.

"Improvise," she said. "The old songs are no good; we have to create our own. Jam. Make it up."

I wasn't Mom. Stepmomdom sucked. So, I decided to become Neo-Mom, a new kind of parent for a changing world.

The first thing Neo-Mom did was accept Kenda's pronouncement: I never tried to take the girls' mother's place. I've always respected the fact that Deb was the one who carried them in her body for nine months, delivered them into the world, fed them in the middle of the night, heard their first words. She and I get along; we've even bonded over men's (well, Bud's) shortcomings. I didn't ask the girls to call me Mom, Mama, Mother, or anything besides Sir—just kidding, Evelyn sufficed. I tried to be their friend, someone they could confide in, but who also got to lay down rules. I'm always flattered when people ask if we're sisters, not just because they must think I'm a decade or two younger than I am and they've compared me to two knockouts, but because, watching them take care of each other (when they're not trying to scratch each other's eyes out), I think it would be a tremendous privilege to be Karlie and Kenda's sibling.

I hadn't read Spock, but I had read the feminist tomes: Carol Gilligan's *In a Different Voice, Reviving Ophelia, The Beauty Myth, Girl Germs*. I knew Karlie and Kenda were reaching that vulnerable age when they would lose all their independence to the monster pressure to Fit In and Look Pretty. I raged like a riot mom when one of the girls told me that she had trouble buying jeans because a relative had said she had "incredibly large hips." The last thing young women need is anything that will give them a complex about their body size; Madison Avenue will take care of that just fine. Inspired by Nadia, Kenda wanted to model. I didn't suppress her, but when she stood uncertainly at casting calls, hiding in her oversized jacket, I didn't push her either. I was glad they got a sense of pop joie de vivre from the Spice Girls. But I was even happier when they preferred Missy Elliott.

Maybe I should have been more a playdates-and-cookies kind of mother (though I think Bud preferred my custom leather pants to an apron). Instead, one weekend I took Karlie and Kenda to Hartford to see the opening of TLC's Fanmail Tour, which I was covering for *Spin*. It was the first time the three of us had traveled alone together: We were girls on a road trip, indulging pop fantasies. Kenda and Karlie were as impressed that we were staying in a hotel where we rode in the elevator with dancers from the show as they were with the big-budget production. They scarfed down nachos at the hotel restaurant and plopped themselves in front of our room's big TV.

I think I learned as much about the state of music from the girls' gut-fueled reaction to Left Eye's outrageous raps (she made fun of having burned down her boyfriend's house) and opening act Destiny's Child's heavily choreographed set as Kenda and Karlie did from my schooled history of hip-hop and R&B. I loved it when T-Boz sang the pop version of *The Beauty Myth*, the anthem "Unpretty": "You can buy all the makeup that MAC can make/But if you can't look inside you/Find out who am I to/Be in a position to make me feel so damn unpretty." Music was changing: It wasn't being made for my demographic anymore; it was for my neo-children. Adapt or die.

I erred most when I slipped out of neo mode and mistook the girls for my own, when I tried to make them what I wanted them to be. You can get away with exerting that kind of control if you're choosing the initial ingredients, but by ages six and eight, the molds have been set. No matter how good a school LESS was, the girls, raised by a high-school dropout, were never going to be academically oriented. After Kenda's initial forays, they didn't care much about the arts either. Or about anything organized or faintly middle class. I've learned to let Bud raise his daughters the way he wants, which is not always the way I want. I've gone from being mad that they weren't taking the right college-prep courses to praying they don't flunk another year. I've had to realize I'm never going to boast about their language skills or concerts to my coworkers, that I should just be glad they're good-hearted and thoughtful (usually) and not likely to become Republicans.

And that they call me their mother.

It actually didn't take that long to earn the m-word. I tried not to make a big deal of it, the first time Kenda introduced me to someone as "my mom." I wasn't sure if she was talking about me or not. Then, she did it again, said, "This is my mom."

Then, it became normal. The longer I was around, the simpler it became for them to give me a title, and "mother" was less confusing and embarrassing than "my dad's girlfriend" or neo-mom. Sometimes, I'm their stepmom; sometimes, I'm their mom. Sometimes, they're my daughters; sometimes, my stepdaughters. Usually, we insert the prefix for matters of clarity. Or, if we're pissed off.

I'm never capital-letter Mom; that's still Deb. They address me as Evelyn. But I have earned the position of mother. They have two of us.

Life has tossed the girls around. I'm an unlikely source for stability. Maybe I've tried too hard to overcompensate for all of us sometimes, at the cost of flexibility. Sometimes, I'm shocked at the clichéd things that come out of my mouth: "Eat your vegetables. Pick up your room. Respect your elders." So much for the rebel girl.

No one would mistake me for a virtuoso, but I think my improvisational mom gut is okay. Mostly, I've been there, for an increasingly long term. That's what has counted. First periods, boyfriends, sex: I gradually got let in on special moments that needed a woman's perspective.

I'll never forget the first time Karlie said, "I love you, Evelyn," or the gratitude in Kenda's eyes one Michigan night when I stayed up with her while she was sick. I don't have a song or a poem for those moments. They just were.

11

Welcome to Miami

∞ ∞ ∞

A year into our New York experiment, I knew it wasn't going to work. Kenda was still saying she wanted to live in Michigan. Karlie was leaving the warm nest of LESS and heading into junior high and all the scary things that entailed. We were all getting on each other's nerves in Big Red, and the Dumbo setup was a logistical disaster. Bud was working hard but still figuring out how to run a carpentry business in a city where there was, more often than not, nowhere to park a van. Neither of us had a steady income, but the two rents were due every month.

So, it seemed providential when my friend Ray told me that the *Miami Herald* was looking for a pop music critic.

San Francisco had taught me that New York had spoiled me for living in most other places. Whenever I grew weary of the Gotham grind, I could think of only three American cities where I wouldn't soon get bored: Los Angeles (as big and busy as New York; plus, I still held onto that California dream), New Orleans (historic and exotic), and Miami (emergent and exotic).

During the last half of the '90s, I visited Miami every year, when the Winter Music Conference (WMC) drew thousands of clubgoers to South Beach's neon, pastel streets. Björk, the Chemical Brothers, Madonna, and Fatboy Slim were helping make electronic music (a.k.a. techno, rave, electronica, house, disco by any other name) the Next Big Thing—or so we thought. That music revolution never quite happened, maybe because we couldn't decide what to call it, or maybe because it was one of those brilliant ideas you have when you're stoned that don't quite withstand the light of day. In Miami, during the world's premiere gathering of dance and electronic music fans and professionals, a lot of us were stoned.

Drugs weren't required. Even chemical-free, it was easy to get a contact high on love and happiness. Many recovering addicts find the sensory stimulation of raves to be a sort of healthy methadone. Whereas a drunk crowd can get ugly and violent, when people tripping on Ecstasy collide in a packed club, they stop and rub each other's backs. All these angsty, high-pressured, New York industry types got all lovey-dovey in Miami. That's why raves are so popular in war-torn areas like Israel, Berlin, America's suburbs: The desperate are self-medicating.

There were WMC moments so comically debauched and/or magical, I wonder if I hallucinated them, such as the time some pasty Englishmen ran naked into the water at Nikki's Beach Club and a seagull tried to take off with their shorts, or the night a group of us were hailing a cab in vain and a bandanaed babe pulled up in her Sebring convertible and became our friend and chauffeur. One day, I waited in line at the Marlin Hotel forever, while multiple simultaneous occupants—male and female—tied up the only two stalls in the women's bathroom. Finally, I sat down to business, only to have the door yanked open by another trio looking for somewhere to do their illicit business. Instead of retreating apologetic and embarrassed, they flirted. "You're cute. Where are you from?" they chatted, as I sat there with my pants around my ankles and my hands covering my red face. This was at 4 p.m.—the night hadn't even begun.

People had bad trips; I had bad trips; one year, someone died. But we took care of each other, talked each other down, made sure we all drank plenty of water. We were there the night Basement Jaxx busted open house music with their cheeky British new wave in a small, sweaty upstairs bar on Washington Avenue. At the Cameo, Roni Size and Reprazent brewed a concoction of frenetic hip-hop, techno, and dub that I called drum 'n' bass 'n' God. DJ Heather made a bed of gospelly, syncopated, classic Chicago house. Ben Watt sifted the sands of Nikki's and unearthed Ibiza. On the rooftop of the Nash Hotel, Little Louie Vega refound disco's Latin groove.

We marveled at the progressive, positively European beneficence of a city that let its clubs stay open late, then turned all the streetlights on and provided ample police protection at closing hour to make sure inebriated late-nighters departed safely. Other cities would have taken a more philistine approach to a party crowd; in fact, in 2004, the idiot then mayor of Miami tried to stop the Ultra Music Festival, Winter Music's big outdoor party. But Miami Beach was cool like dat. Its officials knew WMC was free advertising to a deep-pocketed, cosmopolitan, global crowd. We were all feeling so good, and then the weather was perfect, the sun bounteous and gentle, the ocean wide and blue, the sand soft and warm, the art deco colors like sunrise poured into architecture.

I knew I'd gotten a bent, beatific view of the Magic City, but I fell for it. I jumped at the *Herald* opening. Lead pop critic at the Pulitzer Prize–winning top newspaper in the town that seemed to be the gateway to the twenty-first century: What writer wouldn't want to be that?

Miami would provide two things we needed desperately: space and financial security. It was time to "settle down," if running around in clubs writing about bands can be called settling down. Not to mention the fact that the tech boom had bust. Magazines and websites were folding; book publishers were getting stingy. It was a good time to get out of New York.

I moved first to scout out neighborhoods and real estate. Bud and the girls arrived a few months later, in the middle of August, when the Miami heat and humidity are impossibly oppressive, of an intensity not really to be described. Bud stripped to his boxers and pressed his flesh into the cool tiles of the four-bedroom, three-bathroom 1938 bungalow I had found in the north part of Miami Beach. I cranked the AC.

After Big Red, our bungalow seemed gigantic. The girls had their own rooms and a shared bath, perfect for pubescent sisters. Bud and I had an actual master/mistress suite. There was a living room and a dining room, a front and back yard. I even had an office. Years later, a sister book-club member with an entertainment executive husband and pristine white-tile floors helped put our humble abode in perspective when she looked around and exclaimed, "I like small houses! They're so cute!" By bloated Miami standards, we live in a cottage, but to us, it's Camelot.

When we first visited Miami, Bud and I checked out several neighborhoods. We noticed that while kids played outside and grown-ups chatted on porches in working- and lower-class districts, all the "good" areas seemed barren of people; apparently, the sun fries the upper crust. North Beach is a pass-plates-over-the-fence-kind-of-friendly hood. The area has a mix of cheap apartment buildings and waterfront mansions, with middle-class homes like ours in between. Waves of immigration have brought Brazilians, Cubans, Colombians, and, most recently, Argentineans, gays, bohemians, and yuppies. With yards and picket fences, it can feel suburban—but the houses all have individual character. We call one corner lot with its marlin mailbox and coral turret Spongebob's house. The nonagenarian Cuban immigrant who lives there is a big flirt.

The proximity to water feeds my nature-girl soul. A block from our house, you can stand in two little parks and watch dolphins cavort in the bay. Macaws hang out in our avocado tree; iguanas use the power lines for highways. The ocean, with its reefs, dolphins, stingrays, and sharks, is a mere mile away. Ranging from deep teal to sky blue, the color of the Atlantic in South Florida is legendary.

North Beach is also an urban neighborhood: Miami's not known as a pedestrian city, but we can walk to restaurants, stores, a farmer's market, and a public pool and soccer field (if the inept Miami Beach government would ever finish their renovation). When I was scouting the neighborhood, I noticed there was a maternity center nestled in two little houses a couple blocks north and a bucolic-looking Montessori school just to the east. In the back of my mind, I thought these might come in handy.

Normandy is the kind of place where not only do you know your neighbors, but they become your best friends. After Hurricane Wilma turned our street into a river, knocked out our fruit trees, and stole our power, we gathered in each other's backyards and took turns hosting barbecues. Without TVs and computers, the kids played together, relaxed and imaginative. One night, they created their own entertainment by shining a light on a shaken palm frond and shouting, "Hurricane!"

This isn't South Beach; it's North Beach. Same city, different vibe. If I want clubs and decadence, I just have to get in my car and drive ten miles toward the equator. A few months after we moved, I bought a Mustang convertible so I could make the journey in Sunshine State style. A few years later, we put a pool in the backyard beneath the avocado tree. Stars, cars, bars, sand, sea, swimming: My California dreaming has come true, minus the California part.

One morning, a month after the family's arrival, Bud and I rode our bikes to the ocean. We held each other in the quiet water, savored our good fortune at last, talked about getting married. Maybe, finally, we were going to get a little more of that paradise we first found in the UP. We stopped for *café con leche* and Argentinean pastries at a local restaurant—this was to become a ritual.

When we got home, there was a message from Bud's sister Peggy on the answering machine: Two planes had flown into the World Trade Center.

We turned on the TV and watched as the first tower fell. I couldn't believe what I was seeing, kept saying, "It can't have collapsed; all those firemen in there!" Then I cried. Terrified, we called our friend Debbi, who lived just a few blocks north of Ground Zero. The gorgeous penthouse windows we had always envied gave her a direct view of terror. She had been out jogging when she saw the first plane complete its suicide mission and made it inside just in time to catch number two.

While we talked, she gasped, "Oh my god, the second tower's fallen!" I turned to look at the news and saw on TV the black cloud of smoke and debris that Debbi was watching race across the sky toward her. Afraid the windows would break, she ran into the other room. The glass held firm, but a part of Debbi, who had a new life just germinating in her womb, didn't.

For a few hours, we didn't know where her husband, Sam, racing toward her from Midtown, was. Finally we got the call: He was safe. Then their phones went out. For months Debbi battled depression as she grew big with child. Her husband broke under the stress, too, and secretly started taking drugs. Now, their Tribeca treasure looks out onto blue sky, and Sam doesn't live there anymore.

Jeff watched the towers burn from the roof of our old Dumbo loft. He said you could see the bodies falling. "It was grim. It was unspeakable. You cannot imagine."

No one I knew was killed or injured physically on September 11, but my dear New York friends suffered financially and emotionally for years. I was so glad we weren't there, and yet I had tremendous survivors' guilt.

Kenda and I went back that October. She missed Nadia; I wanted to hold everyone I knew, tell them I loved them. You could still smell the catastrophe all the way up on East 5th: an acrid stench of toxins and hate.

As we waited in the airport to fly back to Miami, I saw on the news that the United States had just bombed Afghanistan. My heart stopped. It was a dark and uncertain time, full of anthrax and shoe-bombers; we didn't know what else terrorists had planned. I told Kenda what was happening and asked if she felt okay flying that day. She said yes, but her eyes were big in her head, a look a child's face should never have. I grabbed her hand and left the airport. We could wait another day to go home.

Bud and I got married September 18, despite—or maybe because of—the audacity of evil. It was a simple ceremony on the southernmost point of Miami Beach, performed by a notary public named Jody, photographed by our new friend Susie, witnessed by the girls and Otis. We had chosen that spot in part because it was supposedly a section of the beach that allowed dogs. It turned out the rules had changed, and mid-ceremony, an officer tried to interrupt our vows and arrest Otie. Susie talked him out of it. Then, when she signed our marriage license, Jody discovered her stamp had expired. Bud and I didn't officially become hitched for weeks. I just couldn't get this marriage thing right!

If it weren't for the girls, I might not have bothered with matrimony round two. After all, Bud and I were both once burned by what we call our "practice marriages." But I wanted to prove to Kenda and Karlie that we weren't moving them around the country for nothing, that I was committed to all this complication too. Not that they leapt for joy when Bud kissed the bride; I was still, perennially, on trial.

After the ceremony, I peeled off my ivory silk dress with embroidered roses to reveal the bathing suit beneath. Ignoring the ancient past this time, Bud carried me over the threshold—well, down the dune—and we dove into the sea.

The New York economy had ground to a halt, but Miami was booming. It seemed like everyone was either a realtor, had an in-

vestment property, or was remodeling—and had money to burn.
Skilled carpenters who spoke English were a valuable commodity,
so Bud had no trouble finding work. It was hard for his practically
Canadian blood to get used to working in the subtropical heat. But
we quickly discovered one of South Florida's greatest assets: You're
never more than a couple hundred feet from a pool, bay, beach, or
lake.

My husband took to Miami like a fisherman to water. He
brought a 1950s aluminum boat down from Michigan. It was to-
tally impractical for Miami since the saltwater ate away the metal,
but the vintage tin Viking was our introduction to the area's life
aquatic. With newcomers' chutzpah, we took that little seventeen-
foot boat all the way down to Biscayne National Park, where it
looked like a sardine can next to the gleaming, hulking fiberglass
hulls of the other weekend campers—there we were, white trash
again. When the Viking's hull became too leaky, we traded up to a
Trophy Bayliner with a cabin beneath the bow that took us all over
this tropical Venetian waterscape: the Atlantic Ocean, Biscayne
Bay, the Intracoastal Waterway, the Miami River, the Coral
Gables Waterway, the Little River.

Bud was gutted when the Trophy got stolen. Then, he decided
it was a sign—time to trade stinkpots for a sailboat. For what we
had spent on a motor for the Trophy, he got a twenty-five-foot
Hunter. He spent weekend after weekend fixing it up. It was his
deer-hunting cabin, fishing boat, Harley, and camper all in one.
Bud took sailing lessons, read books about around-the-world voy-
ages, and pored over knot manuals and mariners' maps.

Films, music videos, award shows, and TV series have ensured
that the whole world knows what Miami looks like. And yet, the

city's more than the beautiful, sinful bimbo it's made out to be. If New York's a mosaic, Miami's a kaleidoscope: a tumble of glass fragments that align into different spectacles each time they're shaken—by a hurricane, race riot, Elian Gonzales, or boatload of Haitian immigrants. Miami's "da bottom" of North America (as it's referred to by rappers), the top of Latin America—a Caribbean outpost in a Confederate state. The anti-Castro politics of Cuban exiles cast a conservative shadow over the multimayor municipality. Meanwhile, men and women promenade through South Beach with thongs and bikinis barely covering their surgically enhanced figures. Bohemians descend from the north to escape the tradition-bound Midwest and New England in limestone Coconut Grove bungalows. Deposed military leaders and working families from South America ascend to find the suburban dream in Mc-Mansions.

They all meet in a place originally built for escapist vacations, not settlement: Sodom by the Sea. I've witnessed grown men howling like dogs at the sight of babes in convertibles, neighbors' flesh distorting like atomic Playdough with successive and excessive surgeries, and P. Diddy dropping a bottle of champagne from a club balcony onto the partiers below while a cuddling Janet Jackson and Justin Timberlake looked on approvingly. Miami is crazy, literally: The population has an unusually high rate of mental illness—and that's not counting the celebrities. Gatsby would have loved it.

Surreal as it can be, 2.36 million people live in Miami–Dade County, and they're not all flossing floozies. Miami houses the best art fair in the Western Hemisphere, one of the top independent bookstores in the country, several film festivals, a globally renowned symphony, two acclaimed ballet companies, the theater that debuted the 2003 Pulitzer Prize winner for drama, several important art museums and collections, the top dance-music conference in the world, multiple reggae festivals, konpa festivals, a Trinidadian carnival, Argentinean rock festivals, and, of course, the Coochie and Crunk Festival. Most South Floridians rarely venture to touristy, tacky Ocean Drive. They prefer the clubs of downtown and the Design District, or not to club at all but to shop at malls, golf, fish, or sail.

At the start of the third millennium, Miami had both the highest poverty rate and the richest-per-density community (Fischer Island) in the country. The stretch Hummers on Ocean Drive glide past the destitute and deranged making their beds in the sand. The art deco hotels where celebs shelter shimmer across the causeway from the dismal Pork and Beans projects where rap stars are born—and where, in 2006, a nine-year-old was shot dead in the neck while playing with a doll on her front porch. Jacki-O, the Chanel-wearing hustler from Liberty City (a.k.a. 1985's McDuffie riots' ground zero), who bragged of boosting (shoplifting) from Bal Harbor's upscale boutiques on her 2004 debut album, filed for bankruptcy a year later.

In the third millennium, Miami is America's wild, glitz-meets-grits frontier, where politicians blow their brains out in newspaper lobbies, an infant is felled by a bullet in a neighborhood likened to Beirut, and disco queens serenade the opening of a $446.3 million Cesar Pelli–designed performing arts center. All our aughties national cultural obsessions—celebrity, cosmetic surgery, bling, reggaeton, terrorism, migration, crime scenes, even the Abramoff lobbying scandal—come home to roost in Da Bottom.

South Florida is a writer's smorgasbord. Culture is in ferment, and I'm an eyewitness of record. I've watched hip-hop erase decades of causeway apartheid by providing South Beach with its next wave of glamour, then caught the cops red-handed, monitoring those rappers. I've raced to the site of Suge Knight's shooting, canvassed a flea market with Russell and Rev. Run Simmons to get out the vote, and waited hours for Missy Elliott to get her hair done so she could cast her first-ever presidential ballot. I've danced under the stars to Yerba Buena's funky *son* and songs at an oceanfront bandshell and packed in with the throngs at a smoky Little Havana club swinging to the Spam All-Stars' mix of Afro-Cuban jams and hip-hop samples. I've been backstage while indie-groove provocateur Peaches and punk legend Iggy Pop planned to make weird music together.

And then, I've gone home and jumped in my pool.

I hated to move the girls again. By the time they finally left New York, Kenda, of course, had decided she loved it there. Karlie never really took to the Big Apple and was happy for a change, she said. But it's never a good thing for kids to get shuffled around so much. Karlie went to five different schools in five years. Just when she had one figured out, it would be time to leave.

The girls were reaching that most self-conscious of ages, especially for girls: pubescence. Sometimes I think we couldn't have picked a worse place to bring two beautiful, relatively innocent young women. Perhaps because there is no season in which you can hide your spreading gut or dimpled thighs behind layers of clothes, Miamians are obsessed with body culture. Fake boobs are everywhere, even on preschool teachers. Small wonder a TV show about plastic surgery is set here or that a world-famous diet is named after South Beach.

Luckily for them, Karlie and Kenda had what it most took to fit in in Da Bottom: natural beauty. They quickly learned to combat the subtropical humidity by greasing and tying back their hair Latina-style, to show off their figures with tight boy-beater tank tops and hip-hugger capris. Blonde and blue eyed, Kenda was ostracized at first for sticking out in the sea of brown (although many of her classmates were simultaneously spending thousands on bleaches, straighteners, contact lenses, and skin creams). Then, she began to get her mother's buxom figure. Now, she could stop a train with her looks. Leggy, lean, and strong, Karlie has no problem passing as Latin, though those green eyes make her unique. With her long locks dyed black and her "yo this" and "yo that," she's left Michigan far behind.

The United States' multilingual future is a reality at Miami Beach High School, where students of dozens of nationalities dine on fast-food lunches amid the din of Spanish in multiple accents, Portuguese, Jamaican patois, Haitian Kreyol, vestigial Valley Girl jargon, and ghetto slang. Karlie and Kenda's friends have Argentinean, Cuban, Venezuelan, Haitian, French, Irish, Peruvian, and Colombian parents. The girls have never studied a language besides English, but, learning by osmosis, they can probably speak a few better than I can.

It took a couple of years, but now they love Miami. Why not: It's Candyland for teens. The girls have mastered the art of being cool. The little kids who thought Will Smith was the height of hip-hop when I met them now have nothing but rap posters on their walls—and Bob Marley. Karlie, still a tomboy, loves crunk, music with that bottom-rattling bass and Southern drawl. Kenda idolizes Tupac.

They awe and frighten me. I don't know what kind of life skills they're learning, how they'll make it when they're eighteen. Sometimes, from my middle-class perspective at least, they seem one step from the edge of delinquency. When they're suspended, in fights, or arrested, that's when I let Bud be the parent.

Fortunately, I have other things to worry about now.

12

Broken Water

❧   ❧   ❧

Bud and I were in a borrowed trailer parked on my old familial property in the Upper Peninsula, when a $12 drugstore science kit prophesied the inevitable future on which I had stopped counting. We watched as two dots turned blue, not slowly but with quick assurance, confirming what my late period and bulging bosom had already told me: I was pregnant.

Even during my dead-baby-joke rebellion phase, I assumed I would be a mother, but I barely imagined it. Or rather, children were background characters in my various life fantasies of romance, adventure, and glory. They would be there, quietly doing their homework in their rooms, while I banged out books on my typewriter. I could see them in the snapshots we'd send home from Victoria Falls, or we'd buy baguettes together in Paris, then hold hands as we walked back to our garret.

I didn't have concrete notions of kids because, before Karlie and Kenda, I'd spent so little time with them. I never had younger siblings, nieces, or nephews. My cousins lived thousands of miles away. With one exception, all the members of my inner circle were childless. Vickie's family was so spectacularly alternative, it was a political statement itself. She and her partner, Linda, had two kids via artificial insemination; the father is a gay Peruvian immigrant. After Linda gave birth to Kali, Vickie was transformed.

"The only way I can describe it is, it's like having a crush," she told me. "Every day I look at this person, and I'm just amazed. I think about her all the time. I can't wait to go home and be with her. It may not be for everyone, but I say, do it."

Tad and I had planned on reproducing. When he ended our relationship, I felt like he killed little Billie and Dusty. I think that's why Bud's girls were so appealing to me: They helped fulfill that empty promise. From the very first weekend we met, Bud won me over with talk of the rewards of parenting, how he'd like another kid, what a great mom I would be. "Unconditional love." That phrase wouldn't leave my head.

Infertility was not a problem. I'd known since my mid twenties, when years of careful birth control went awry one night, that the baby-making machinery was working. Too early in my relationship with Bud, I got pregnant again. I never regretted either abortion, although I woke up from the second one sobbing. Having watched friends, from a teenager to a grown mother of three, make the same decision, I know most women don't decide to terminate a pregnancy any more lightly or quickly than they decide to have kids.

Once our lives were on the same page, let alone in the same state, Bud and I tried procreating again. And again and again. After a couple years, I tried not to think about missed opportunities. We didn't get all repro-crazy, didn't see a fertility doctor or have sex when my temperature rose. I didn't need to be a biological mother to feel complete; I had just hoped for it as a bonus.

Bud says he knew the minute we conceived. It was almost four years to the day from our abortion. We had moved to Miami; it was a hot summer night. "That was a baby-making load," he whispered in my ear as we lay sweating on our bed. He likes to say stuff like that, talk that's at once dirty and romantic, corny and sexy. Sometimes, I wonder if he thinks he's a porn star. Me, I had stopped thinking about babies. It was the summer the girls were hitting puberty, and Miami Beach was bouncing and shaking to a hip-hop invasion; I had enough on my hands.

Then, my breasts began bulging like an anime princess's. It was summer, and I was at my twentieth high school reunion. Cindy was there too, also newly pregnant, with her third child, which she was still keeping secret. Our respectively known and possible laden states kept us from toasting the old days with the ritual reunion intoxication, but it was almost as much fun to have this shared conspiracy, to whisper about the idea of what was in our bellies and forecast future playdates. They would have to be transcontinental playdates, since Cindy lived in Oregon. Part of me wanted to tell all the widening cheerleaders and balding jocks that I was with child. What's a reunion for if not a little bragging? But I also liked being the one who didn't have kids, who had made it as a writer, traveled the world, lived in Miami Beach.

A week later, the early pregnancy test made its two-dot revelation.

Being pregnant, I felt like a drag queen who had found a killer beehive wig. I had spent my life thinking about the amazing things women were capable of if given half the chance: rap, fly, legislate, drum, write, paint, give orders, compute. But beyond avoiding it like the plague, I hadn't thought much about this basic thing that almost all of us could do, but no man could: grow a life inside our bodies. Pregnancy's rush of hormones brought a female power that didn't depend on consensus, editors, amplifiers, or theory. I milked that power (so to speak).

My relationship to my own body changed; I became wedded to my flesh in new, weird, painful, awful, and awesome ways. I loved being a pawn of nature, watching my lifelong skinny self swell to voluptuous dimensions. I haven't always been in touch with my body's feminine qualities. For instance, breasts: Mine have always been rather unremarkable, by which I mean to say small. As the nine months of gestation passed, these previously overlooked body parts took on a life of their own, like some science fiction fantasy of an adolescent boy. Kelis was singing my theme song, "Milk-shake." Who needs implants when you got milk?

I had breasts, and damn it I was going to use them. I took my cue from the hot Latin mamas around me, who let their bellies push out between tank tops and low-rider pants. I eschewed maternitywear's frumpy stretch slacks, billowy blouses, and dresses with the voluminous appeal of Home Depot tarpaulins in favor of bright knit outfits from Argentina that hugged my bumps and curves. I found a muse in Deb Ohanian, a sometime promoter who, a few years earlier, had made history by bringing the Cuban band Los Van Van to Miami, inciting protests. When she wasn't provoking the city's old-guard politics, Deb made clothes for expectant mothers. Her black chiffon slacks, sheer leopard-print tops, tropical sundresses, and white halter top with a cartoon drawing of the Chrysler building were their own invitation to riot. I posed in them, wearing red boxing gloves, for a *Herald* fashion spread we titled "Knocked-up Knockout."

I loved having a stomach, too, not having to worry about being skinny. Writing, I would find myself lost in thought, rubbing my Buddha belly. This navel-gazing would get interrupted by sudden movement: The baby was moshing in the pit again. Even as a fetus, Cole was a little acrobat. You could see his feet poking out as he hung from my rib-cage monkey bars. I'd tickle them, tickle me.

It was hard to keep my hands off this elastic, spastic wonder that my body had become—for me at least. Men perennially complain that women stop having sex after they have kids, but they don't often mention their own paralyzing fear of the volcanic forces that their partners' bodies become when seeded. I have heard men admit that they're afraid sex will hurt the baby, a "gut" response with no scientific basis or balls. Their loss; maybe it was part of the hormone upheaval, but expecting a child made me horny as hell.

Pregnancy wasn't all hipness and bosomy pride. I suffered some morning sickness. Worse for me was the mucus factory. With my body retaining the water it would later so reluctantly let go of, my sinuses became perpetually clogged. By the ninth month, I was blimplike and increasingly miserable. I couldn't sleep on my stomach, sides, or back—in other words, I couldn't sleep. My calves cramped at night. I peed every hour or so. In retrospect, I suspect that my bladder's impatience was nature's way of getting me used to getting up for nighttime infant feedings. Thanks, Ma.

Most women's water breaks when they're about to have a baby. The membrane holding the fluids in which the fetus has been bathing rends, the inside pours out, and a grown woman suddenly wets herself. The cliché is that this happens with such stealth, it takes the hapless lady by surprise, say, in the canned-fruit aisle of a grocery store. "Water breaking" is an apt metaphor for the parenting transformation, for an experience that entails rapid immersion, soul cleansing, and public embarrassment. Children heave a big rock into the middle of our liquid beings. But water doesn't break into pieces; it flows back together.

And then, there are those of us whose water must be broken for them. Not surprisingly, given the dilly-dallying route I had taken to get to this point, I did not deliver my child into this world easily. I don't know if it was Cole resisting life by doing a backbend or me resisting motherhood by refusing to open wide, but the midwife had to break my amniotic sac, and the baby got stuck.

We were at the North Beach maternity center, the sweet complex just a couple blocks from home. I had spent the previous eight months regularly visiting one of its two houses, the one with the kitchen offices and bedroom exam rooms. Shari and her students checked my blood sugar, belly circumference, and weight, along with the baby's position and, my favorite part, heartbeat. I still have a tape of that whooshing and rolling rhythm, not a contained percussive sound like that of a born human but more tribal, less techno.

For the birth, I graduated to the second house, where the bedrooms were decorated with tropical fish, jungle prints, or girlie lace that hid oxygen canisters in the corners. A makeshift walkway connected the office building to the birthing building's screened porch, where two hot tubs sat. I was all about the hot tubs.

Considered radical by some (like Dad), the maternity center was actually a compromise decision. Shari would have been happy to do a home birth, but that was a little too comfy for me. Discreet as they were, I wanted those oxygen tanks, to feel that, if needed, the tools of the trade were close at hand. Besides, Shari was allergic to fur, and our place was the House of Fur.

The birthing center was like a commune. In fact, it doubled as Shari's home. The waiting room was her living room; sometimes she'd walk into the examining room and pull clothes out of the closet. There were always lots of other mothers, kids, and mid-wives-in-training about. The clientele was a mix of rich bohemians, Orthodox Jews, and indigent women who could afford Shari's budget prices. On the wall were pictures of past clients: naked women caressing their bulging bellies or holding newborns, Madonnalike. You could watch videos of center births, wonderful, happy, drug-free affairs where the men held their naked wives in a tub, and, panting and groaning and breathing, the women delivered underwater.

Maybe this hippie central was a strange place for a punk like me. Definitely, the mellow placidness of some of the women, who wore their noisily sucking babies in slings, drove me crazy. But far more repellent to me than the scent of patchouli was the idea of an antiseptic, clinical, cold birth. I had visited one doctor when I was searching for a place to have Cole. Sitting in his hospital office, on hard chairs, reading the usual magazines and waiting to be called in by the nurse, I felt like I'd felt in a hundred doctor's offices before: like something was wrong with me. But nothing was wrong with me. Quite the opposite.

The modern human condition of alienation and disassociation begins at birth. We're brought into this world on drugs fed to us umbilically, by hands covered with plastic gloves, under fluorescent lights, surrounded by machines and strangers, maybe with some bad, tinkly, New Age muzak piped in. That's not what I wanted for my kid. I wanted candles, sobriety, friendly faces, and PJ Harvey (even though, as it turned out, I would not be "Happy and Bleeding").

I also wanted to test myself. Women have been delivering babies without drugs since the dawn of time. I didn't want to be a modern wuss. Did the person who had slammed to Tribe 8 and had three tattoos need anesthesia? It was okay to take horse tranquilizers in nightclubs but not painkillers at birth centers, I reasoned. Go figure.

So I sat cross-legged on the floor while a long-haired sling mama showed my birthing class how to nurse, and while Shari explained what we could do with our placentas (dining or gardening, anyone?). The bulletin boards were covered with Polaroids of recent parents and children. As our dates neared, we saw the faces of former classmates. During one sad session, Shari confirmed the rumor that a baby had not made it. Death is a grim reality of the birthing process; still, I felt a pall over a place sensitive to bad vibes.

Cole could have been born on 3/3/3, but he was late. Shari called me into the maternity center on a Sunday to see what the holdup was. Tamra, my neighbor from down the block and fellow former Wisconsinite, was there also. She was late, too, only this was her third child, so she was far more relaxed about it than I. A number of our classmates were past our due dates; Shari worried that we were all going to pop at once. She rubbed some primrose oil on my cervix, told me to have a good romp with Bud (sex is known to induce labor), and sent me home.

That night, just as I was getting ready for bed, I felt my first cramp.

Within two hours, the waves of pain were coming hard and regular, and I was wimping out. Instead of staying home and getting the sleep I would need for the difficult job ahead of me, I went to the center. Maybe I was impatient to be a mama. Maybe I just wanted to be with some natural-birth professionals, instead of my excited, but vaguely panicked, family. Mostly, I was thinking of the hot tub.

Which turned out to be a bad idea. Sure, lying in it, listening to Björk, and feeling the warm Florida air waft through the screens and the pain subside was bliss. But with the pain went my labor. Every time I soaked, I stopped dilating. And little ol' me needed to dilate.

Compounding matters, Tamra had gone into labor shortly before I had, and she was having a home birth. Shari was shuttling back and forth between us. Every time Shari left, my labor would slow. My water wasn't breaking; Cole wasn't descending; I never did get the urge to push. I was starting to feel like a failure—and to freak out. In case Tamra and I decided to deliver at the same time, Shari called in her backup midwife, a woman I had only met once. So much for a familiar face.

Then, Harry met Shari: Tamra's first son and Cole's future playmate was delivered, without problem, at home. Shari came back to the center and got to work on me—exhausted, hungry, hurting, scared me.

I didn't feel like pushing, but push I did. We had long ago given up the hot tub. I was in one of those cute little rooms, so out of it, I don't know what the decor was. Bud was there, an experienced but nervous male in women's territory. The girls—excited, disgusted by the sight of me naked, and rather mind-blown—were in and out. Mom, who had flown in from California for a month, wanted to help. Shari asked her to count Cole's heartbeats, which were being monitored on one of those blessed machines I'd wanted nearby just in case. I think she meant to keep Mom busy and distracted. The tactic backfired when those heartbeats began skipping.

That's when we all hit hyperspace. Failing heartbeats: This was officially a crisis. Oh god, I started to cry, my baby might die. It had been fourteen hours since I started labor, fourteen hours that I knew were going to be hard, but not like this. Shari told Bud to get on my stomach and push like he was shoving an overpacked suitcase closed. Meanwhile, she was pulling way up where I didn't know hands could reach. We could see Cole's head, covered with dark hair, but for some reason he was doing a backbend—not an ergonomic fetal-delivery position. Mom, Kenda, and Karlie (bless them!) were holding my hands and coaxing, "Come on, Evelyn. You can do it!" I was still in labor and already the refrain from a children's story was running through my delirious brain: I think I can, I think I can, choo-choo! I wanted drugs, forceps, a C-section, a hacksaw: I wanted everything I had philosophically stood against twenty-four hours earlier. "Call the doctor, call the doctor!" the "Words and Guitar" of Sleater-Kinney screeched in my head. Was this me, naked, fat and screaming? How the hell did I get here?

Then, with the help of a little slice of the knife where I once had a perineum (*that* wasn't on the video!), something—or someone—gave. Stubbornly coming forehead instead of crown first, a seven-pound infant yogi emerged from my aching nookie. Shari quickly made sure all his parts were in place, then placed my baby boy in his mama's arms.

Cole wasn't crying, squishy, or covered in blood or poop. As if his—our—heart had never faltered, his eyes looked straight into mine, not questioning but assured—like the newborn know-it-all had already been in the world a thousand years, like he was aware of who I was and where he was, like all it would take was for his body to look a little less like a tadpole and he would be a fully formed human, complete with decided opinions, off-color jokes, and bad hair days. Considering what he had just been through, I didn't expect that look to be so fully sentient, the unequivocal announcement of the unique template of Cole. It's the same look I've seen almost every day since—all my nurture-over-nature arguments took a powerful beating in that divine moment.

Shari, a devout Jew and old-school feminist who has delivered well over ten thousand babies, believes the soul enters the body at birth. Ten-second-old Cole on Mama's breast rooting for milk: soul to soul.

Once Cole was born, it was time for my newfound endowment to go to work. I wanted so badly to be a natural mother. But natural didn't come natural. We tried, from that first moment Cole was born, to breast-feed. I followed the midwife's instructions carefully, offered Cole alternating nipplage on a strict schedule, hired a lactation consultant, positioned the "boppy" nursing pillow just so. (Boppy? Who comes up with these terms?) Cole would lock his lips around my aureole and gaze rapturously up at my face—sweet heaven, that gaze.

He looked like he was feeding, but he didn't seem to be getting anything out. Despite hours spent in position, night and day, he kept losing weight. My overfull breasts went from big to humungous, from boobylicious to excruciatingly painful. Something was very wrong.

I know a lot of women who have tried unsuccessfully to nurse. Bud was allergic to milk, even his mother's. The girls' mother tried to breast-feed but couldn't; neither could mine. Mom admits she didn't try very hard. In her day, bottle-feeding was considered a modern, healthy alternative to the "primitive" breast. Like the denigration of midwives, the promulgation of infant formula was another way the twentieth-century scientific establishment took power away from women. Nursing is natural, but it's also learned, passed on from mother to daughter. That chain had been broken for at least a generation, in my family and most American families. I didn't grow up watching women breast-feed. Once again, here I was, improvising.

Support from others was circumspect and awkward. Mom stood by helplessly, reliving her own bumbled past, as I tried to figure out how these damn sacks worked. Bud wanted to do what he did with the girls: give him a bottle. These two loved ones admired my perseverance, but I think they thought I was crazy. I dyed my hair, experimented with pharmaceuticals, liked music made with synthesizers. Why was I getting all organic now?

After a week, we went to the midwife. She took one look at my skinny baby and whipped out a bottle. For this nursing nazi to turn to artificial nipples, things had to be bad. Shari told us Cole needed to be force-fed high-nutrition formula on the hour or be hospitalized and put on an IV. Until we could get him back in shape, she banned him from my breast.

Watching Cole suckle a bottle while others held him, I wanted to die. Even though it hadn't been working from a nutritional standpoint, nursing had forged a deep emotional and hormonal bond between us. I loved breast-feeding like I loved dancing, swimming, fucking, and reading. But now, a big, black, scary-looking pump sucked the milk from my useless udders while others cradled my child in their arms. I felt like a cow.

Worse was my panicked awareness of Cole's mortality: First, his heart starts skipping in delivery; now this. Years ago, before I left for college, my grandmother sat me down for a heart-to-heart about the importance of faith and family.

"The worst thing that ever happened to me was losing my daughter," Mama said, referring to Mom's only sister, Louise, who died of cancer. "It's bad losing your parents, and your husband, but you expect it. You never want to outlive your own children."

Mama was crying. She didn't get sad and serious like that often. Her words had always haunted me, and, now, I was feeling their full weight: an awful, terrifying fear and ache. I had experienced a lot of depression, some of it self-indulgent wallowing, some of it the inevitable result of divorces and other disappointments. Those first few days of having Cole torn from my chest while I worried that my maternal failure had starved him were a unique hell. I don't know how parents survive the loss of their children. I pray I will never know.

We still don't know what went wrong. Shari described it as something like "failure-to-suck syndrome." (With any luck, Cole will often fail to suck in the future, but hopefully in a less life-threatening fashion.) He had no such problem with the special bottles we used and quickly regained his weight on formula.

As soon as I could, I put him back on the boob.

I don't know if I've ever been as determined in my life as I was to breast-feed my child. A deep-seated feeling of being cuddled, coddled, and cradled was something I always felt I missed out on, despite my parents' abundant love. I was brought up with a very middle-class American fear of the body. We all sat in our separate armchairs and beanbags watching TV, not huddled on the couch. That great yearning feeling wasn't a legacy I wanted to pass on to my son. The patriarchy wasn't going to whip me this time. Cole was going to be a mothersucker if it killed me. At two to three feedings a night for almost a year, it nearly did.

It wasn't easy. My breasts were often full and painful. We developed thrush, kept passing it back and forth, until I finally painted my nipples and his mouth with a cheap kind of iodine called gentian violet that stained everything purple. I'd whip out my lavender tit and shove it into his face, which looked like it had been smeared with grapes. The gargoyle eagles of the Chrysler Building would peer around his blond curls as his head rested on my left arm. I didn't care who saw. I was doing one of the most basic things on the planet, and I was tired of paying the price for it's being suppressed.

As a kid, I was a shirtless tomboy running through sprinklers. As a young woman, I marched down Fifth Avenue for top-freedom. As a mama, I sat bare-breasted in restaurants, malls, and even one work meeting. Nothing was going to stop me again from suckling my child.

It worked. Cole became a healthy, breast-fed baby, an attached-at-the-nipple mama's boy pumped full of nature's best immune system. Once we started, it was hard to stop. Some people thought I was insane to nurse as long as I did. After all, by his fourth month of life, I was working full-time. This meant that, on more than one occasion, I had to run into the port-a-potty at some rock show and pump milk out of my cup-runneth-over breasts. My planned year of nursing grew to fifteen months. I headed out of town for a jam-band festival to finally break his/our habit and wean. My full-to-bursting mammaries made me unusually popular among the laidback longhairs with earth-mother complexes.

I think those gallons and gallons of nature's finest—delivered in reassuring flesh-to-flesh contact, not sucked out of plastic—were one of the best gifts I could give my child. And Cole gave me something precious in return: He made me feel like a natural woman.

13

Bringing Up Baby

Before Cole was born, I could count on one hand the number of diapers I had changed in my life. I tried babysitting a few times when I was a teenager, but I was only in it for the money and, frankly, was better at raking leaves. In retrospect, I can't imagine why any of those parents trusted clueless me with their kids. Maybe it was because one couple were pot dealers. They would leave me and my friend with their young kids, their killer stereo, and a couple of joints, while they went out to party. Robin and I would stick our charges in their beds, get stoned, and listen to Frank Zappa and Bootsy. Thus went the '70s.

My maternal instinct lay somewhere on the human-factory floor next to my ability to knit and cook. Babies made me hapless; I didn't know how to hold them, know how to fold them. Some single women volunteer to watch their friends' offspring. I just had cats.

When Cole came along, I wondered if I could train him to use a litter box.

Liberal mothers with decided, alternative views of how to raise kids populate South Florida's upscale boho hoods (palm tree-studded Miami Beach and the limestone bungalows of Coconut Grove). Their progressive mandates include organic foods (no sugar), nursing slings (not strollers), wooden toys (never plastic), educational books (no TV), Mozart (no rhythms faster than a heartbeat), family beds (no cagelike cribs), and private Waldorf or Montessori schools (no standardized testing). I surrounded myself with these paragons of parenting as Cole gestated, was born, and grew. Their savvy, wisdom, sophistication, and style enthralled me. Some of them had careers, though I was stunned to find how many had stopped working to have kids. Most had successful first marriages so started their families a little earlier than I and were already on their second or third kid. None had erstwhile lumberjack husbands and wayward teenage step-daughters.

The societal pressure to conform multiplies when you repro-duce. No one is more subject to general opprobrium than a mother: It's one thing to be a bad girl, quite another to be a bad mom. A mama's every act of self-indulgence, experimentation, he-donism, narcissism, and rebellion is met with a collective tsk-tsk. At times, I feel like the very essence of my being is on trial.

The alt-moms gave me a community of support without trying to shove me into an apron. They backed me if I wanted to, as one of them so endearingly put it, "have both breasts out and blazing, double-barreled and nursing." They gave me invaluable pediatri-cian and preschool tips and introduced me to the wonder of Robeez soft-leather toddler shoes. They were well informed, progressively minded, kind hearted, well-off. And, sometimes, they could be coparenting nazi snobs.

There's nothing more annoying than a righteous parent. My family of five can't afford to shop at health-food stores (besides, Karlie packed bags at one and came home with stories of protein-deprived, neurotic customers and pimply teens wiping food-prep areas with dirty rags). Slings remind me of peasant skirts; plus, they hurt my swollen udders. Yes, I limit TV, but eliminate it? I'm a pop culture critic; wouldn't that be like cutting my own throat? Mozart was useful for putting Cole to sleep, but my heart still swells with maternal pride remembering the day my son sat in the back of the Mustang and sang along to LCD Soundsystem's electro anthem "Daft Punk Is Playing at My House," shouting along with the hiccupping, probably drunk James Murphy, "My house, my house!" as we neared our bungalow.

I wanted to be a taste-making, trend-setting, world-peace-promulgating parent, but I eventually realized that that form of do-goodism entailed its own conformist pressure. As my friend Susie said to me, as I struggled to "do the right thing," to cover my crazy life with some veneer of normalcy: "Parenting isn't making us straighter. Harry and I seem to be settling into our eccentricities as we get older."

Almost by default, I found myself choosing the alternative to the alternative. Ergonomic strollers and feng shui cribs were like indie rock, I realized: the epicurean choices of elite consumers. Using brown, baggy organic diapers was like trying to tie tofu around Cole's butt. Noggin, the commercial-free channel for preschoolers, was my friend. Cole's TV time didn't replace story time, but *Dora the Explorer* did keep him occupied while I perused the newspaper in the morning.

For the most part, by the time he was one, I put aside the books, websites, and magazines advising me how to cultivate the fruit of my loins. After all, a rather Hallmarkesque miracle happened when Cole was placed in my arms: A language my clumsy body had never studied awoke. I don't know if the midwife dislodged some dormant instinct when she was rooting around in there or what, but from that moment on, most baby tasks came naturally. I clipped nails, wiped butt, massaged, played peek-a-boo, made rice cereal, and crooned nursery lullabies and Velvet Underground songs ("If you close the door, the night could last forever"). It's like the rest of life: You figure it out as you go along. By the time your kid's ready for the next stage, you are too.

I tried to be creative in my discipline, especially since time-outs and spankings just made Cole wilder. One day, when we were returning from the zoo with a classmate and his mother, Cole, overtired, was growing increasingly hostile and hysterical in the back seat. It was December and the first year Cole, at age two, knew what Christmas was. He was already telling the story of how we'd hear something outside, and he'd say, "What's that?" and we'd go outside, and we'd see reindeer tracks, and we'd go inside, and there would be presents, and Santa would have been there, and we'd be happy!

Desperate to return a level of calm to my friend's black-leather-interiored SUV, I warned Cole that Santa wouldn't bring him presents if he wasn't a good boy.

"I don't care," he said.

I whipped out my cell phone, pretended to dial, and said, "Hi, Santa? Hello, how are you? It's Cole Shankle's mom. How's Mrs. Claus? Good? Tell her I say hi.

"Listen, I'm calling because I wanted to let you know that Cole's not being a good boy. I know, it's disappointing, but he just won't listen to me. So, you don't have to bother bringing him any presents for Christmas. That's right, you can give those to some other little boy. If Cole decides to be a good boy, I'll let you know. All right. Sorry to have to bother you."

Cole was quiet for a minute, the anguish of making a moral decision wrenching his rugrat features. Then, he said, "I don't want any presents. I want to be a bad boy!" And he started screaming again.

Cole may have suffered for my improvisation. When, at a childbirth-prep class at the maternity center, a midwife explained the concept of the family bed, I figured, no way. Sure, every now and then Cole could sleep with us, but Bud and I were way too selfish to give up our sex space.

Then we had the nursing crisis. Cole had to be fed regularly; at 3 a.m., that was much easier to do if I could just roll over and slip him tit. I figured he would eventually sleep through the night, in his own bed, even if I had to let him cry it out. The alt-moms, however, explained that this "Ferberizing" (named for the guy who wrote the book on the subject) was cruel and un-p.c. I didn't need much convincing; I was a sucker for Cole's tears. Bud was worse than I was. He would talk tough about not spoiling our little midget, but when it was up to him, Cole always wound up nestled between us.

Our unplanned drift into the family bed has left Cole with lousy sleeping habits. He fights falling asleep, hates to miss out on any possible action, cries to nestle in my armpit. He wakes up in the middle of the night and can't "self-soothe," as Ferber says, so even if he's started the night in his bed, he finds his way to ours. I keep saying he'll grow out of this nocturnal habit. And I keep waiting, bleary eyed.

I've never liked sleeping alone. When Brett was moved out of the room we shared as toddlers, I replaced him with my cat, Brendalyn, who would crawl under the covers and dream in my arms. A year or so later, I saw a werewolf movie. Terrified, I had nightmares, and my parents let me sleep with them for a month. I still remember the bliss of waking up between their bodies, how rejected I felt when they sent me back to my own bed. Private bedrooms are a luxury and burden of a flush, industrialized society. They're not necessarily best for kids seeking love and security—though they do make parents' love lives easier.

At night, we all arrange ourselves on the king bed so we're just within reach. Sometimes I wake up with Cole's legs over mine, the cat Moonpie purring against my back, Otis on my feet, Bud somewhere over there, my immobilized back aching. I reach out and caress everyone, feel their sleeping bodies lean into my hand. Then, others-soothed, I go back to sleep.

I was better at this family stuff than I thought I would be. Still, it helped that I had Team Cole: not a village, but an ad hoc posse. Half of my job seems to be organizing parenting, rather than actually doing it. It's the same with meals: I can think up a menu and buy the ingredients, but it's best if Bud cooks.

I like the sound of coparenting, the way the word implies a non-gender-defined sharing of labor. My husband, having been through this twice already, is a baby-burping pro. He's the kind of dad who's not only unafraid to change a diaper but can do it in a flash, whipping a disgusting Pamper off, wadding it into a ball, rim-shotting it into the Diaper Genie, and wrapping the next one on, while I would still be painstakingly trying not to get my fingers dirty. Bud could enfold Cole in a tight little blanket burrito that defied my manual skills. Showering, he'd hold onto the slippery little newborn with one hand and soap himself with the other, while I hovered, panicked Cole would drop. Bud took care of Cole at night when I was out covering shows. I'd come home with my ears ringing to find they'd fallen asleep together on the bed, father and son watching a cowboy movie.

Nonetheless, despite Bud's egalitarian efforts, I wind up taking on the greater burden of responsibility, work, and control in raising Cole. That's generally fine with me: Cole's Bud's third child and my one and only. Bud's in charge of the girls; I want to be in charge of the boy. The older Cole gets, the more issues of schooling and cultural enrichment (a fancy term for zoos and museums) become central, the more Cole's raising rests on my shoulders.

I'm sure traditional sexism plays a role in this division of labor. Not many families have our peculiar circumstances, yet even among Cole's advanced playmate community, the women are almost always the ones who take the kids to the playground. Bud's years of single-parenting put him in touch with his feminine side, yet he's still in many ways an übermale. The day Hurricane Wilma tore our yard apart, his friend Bill came over and dropped off his son, and the two dads disappeared in Bill's Jeep for hours, checking on Bud's boat and "touring" the wreckage of Miami—leaving me to watch the boys and girls and get prepared for days without power.

I was beyond livid when they came back. "That's not the kind of woman you married," I reminded Bud, "the kind that placidly stays at home and minds the kids while you're out having a good time."

He looked sheepish and wisely kept his ass put for a couple days.

Sometimes, I think the guys want to help but just don't know what to do. Around the time of Cole's birth, Bud poured all his anxieties into his new boat. While I was trying desperately to nurse, Mom was giving Cole baths, and our son was shriveling up, Bud spent the days outside washing his (literal) Trophy. A friend's husband decided that the night their first son was born was the night he needed to alphabetize their entire CD and LP collection.

At times like these, I realize I suffer from what so many wives throughout the centuries have endured: useless husband syndrome. On really bad days, I refer to men as "sperm providers." Not donors: heaven knows, we don't get it for free.

Fortunately, I had other help. I was always happy to be the prodigal daughter who left home and created her own place in the world. Then Cole came along, and I found myself longing for free familial child care that was not a thousand or more miles away. Mom stayed with us for a month when Cole was born and has returned once a year. Watching her bathe her first grandchild was a revelation for me. I don't remember ever before seeing my accomplished, rational mother cooing in baby tongue, singing little songs, and rubbing her nose in an infant's neck to find the sugar all babies hide there. Of course, I realized, she had bathed Brett and me like that, a few decades earlier. I was witnessing a tender, domestic side of Mom that I only remembered subconsciously, that had become buried under years of lectures, lessons, and unhappiness. I think my son awoke her maternal instinct too. We were all the better because of him.

Quickly on Mom's heels came Dad. The great sentimentalist had nearly had a heart attack when I told him I was pregnant. We were all on speakerphone; I swear he started hyperventilating. Judy finally said they would call back when Dad could form a word. After Cole was born, Dad tried to see him four times a year. The word "doting" doesn't do his feelings for Cole justice. "Papa," as Cole calls him, and his grandson have a special relationship. They move at the same pace, in slow wonder at the world. Dad doesn't have a great handle on the practicalities of taking care of Cole, but, fortunately, his wife, Judy, who never had a kid but taught second grade, does. When they come stay at a local trailer park in their motor home, they always take their grandson for an overnight, giving Bud and me a much-needed evening to ourselves (typically, we have dinner, then fall asleep). They've been generous beyond words, making sure their only grandchild has a head start on the world by paying for most of Cole's preschool tuition.

Bettie Lou is a sympathetic well of wisdom and advice. She tells stories of her psychic bond with her children—how she always could sense, even from hundreds of miles away, when they were hurt or in trouble. Before Cole was born, the skeptic in me doubted these paranormal tales. Now, I know just what she means.

Before Cole was born, Karlie came to me and said, "I can't wait for you to have your baby. Then, there will be one more thing in this world I can love." They may groan and ask for money, but Bud and I can always count on Cole's sisters to watch their brother if we have to run to the store or go out on a date. Sometimes, they're jealous. Every time we buy Cole a toy, Kenda wants to know what we got her. He can be a little brat right back at them. Wanting his parents to himself, he'll order his sisters out of the room in which we're watching *Shrek*, shouting, "Bad boys, no!" Kenda's the most willing to babysit, yet for months he insisted on calling her Karlie—well, "Darlie" (K's a hard sound for "Dolie"). Still, they have to admit, he can be a crackup. He likes to go out to his biggest sister's room (the garage studio), knock on her door, and play with her guinea pig. With their fair coloring, Kenda and Cole most resemble each other. Bud says Cole's a lot like his middle sibling was when she was his age: difficult, demanding, and hilarious.

When we came home from the maternity center, Otis promptly positioned himself under the bassinet and wouldn't move as long as Cole was in there. He essentially hasn't left. He sleeps wherever Cole sleeps, under his bed or at the foot of ours. Our tough-guy Yorkie won't walk around the block unless Cole is with us, follows his little master around the pool with Energizer Bunny endurance. Possessed of the patience of Job, the dog lets Cole pull his hair, crawl over his back, chase him around the house. Every morning when Otie sees us stirring, he jumps on the pillows and licks our faces awake. Boy's best friend.

Our cat God died of cancer the year before Cole was born. Roses, her favorite flower, grow out of her backyard grave. Our other cat, Elvis, slept with us all at night, as she had with me for sixteen years, then died of a stroke when Cole was two. We adopted two neighborhood strays. Paleface is a cutup and hard-ass; Moonpie's the most affectionate cat I've ever had. At night, she throws her purring body into Cole's little hand as he leans across my belly and falls asleep while gently touching her.

I went back to work when my maternity leave ran out, three months after Cole was born. I didn't want to—I would have preferred to freelance rather than go back to an office or take the civilized year of paid leave such advanced countries as Canada and Sweden provide—but we couldn't afford for me to stay home. We were fortunate to find two women who took alternating, loving care of Cole in those formative days.

Lucy was a high-strung Colombian who could make Cole laugh uproariously. One day when he was not even six months old, we were at a little folk concert in Michigan, and the band began playing "Besame Mucho." Cole went crazy, bouncing up and down, trying to dance. I realized he recognized the old bolero, that Lucy sang it to him as she moved around the house, trying to clean up the endless mess of an ex-woodsman, his teenage daughters, their bohemian neo-mom, and a little rugrat.

Rosa's is one of those heartbreaking stories of which Miami is full. Her father spent time in Castro's jails before the family found exile in Venezuela. Of poor health since she was born, Rosa lost two children as infants. Only her daughter Dolce, now a college student, survived. She and her husband moved to Miami when their girl was a baby; a few months later, he died of cancer. Robbed of, or distanced from, so much of her own family, Rosa has an extraordinary amount of love to give. I credit Cole's gentleness, imaginative play, and idiosyncratic use of English to Rosa.

She taught him Spanish and how to garden. When he turned two, he began replying to "I love you" not by saying "I love you too" but with "I love you too much." It was a technically wrong translation of the Spanish phrase *Te amo mucho*, but it made absolute sense.

I used to assume that if I were going to have kids, I would have two. My brother had been my companion on cross-country trips and first teacher of all things rock 'n' roll. Cole was such a source of joy and love, I wanted another one.

One day, I tried talking to my spouse about having a second kid. He got a stricken look on his face, his knuckles turned white on the steering wheel, and he almost ran into the car in front of us.

Bud was finished breeding. He had two daughters and one son; he was forty-three and spent, ready for his midlife second adolescence (which, in Bud's case, manifested itself as an obsession with a boat, not a sports car). I had to admit that adding to our caretaking load wasn't practical. Working full-time and raising two teenage girls and a toddler boy, Bud and I were tired all the time. We weren't as young as we used to be. We were just barely keeping it together.

I didn't want Cole to become a spoiled, lonely, only child. I knew he needed to learn to socialize with kids his age, to share his toys and stop biting whenever another kid got in his way, so I began taking him to parent-and-child classes when he was less than a year. At first, I admit, they were more for me than for him: a way to meet other mothers who lived in my area. I quickly realized I was the only mom who thought the *Kindermusik* classes should have a hip-hop segment. Invitations to playdates and parties did not come streaming our way. Poor Cole was going to have to suffer the consequences of having an unconventional mom.

Cole started school at twenty-one months, not because I was setting him off on a path to Harvard but because I figured that since we had to pay for child care, he might as well get some socialization and learning out of our investment. The Montessori school down the street beckoned with its flower gardens, French doors, wood floors, and butterfly sculptures. It was the prettiest school I'd seen in the whole city, and I'm a sucker for aesthetics.

Mariposa Montessori had a formidable reputation. It was only a few years old, but already it drew the cream of the crop from Miami Beach's wealthy neighborhoods: club owners, models, doctors — rich, beautiful people. If you could even get on it, there was a waiting list. Cole's parent-and-child teacher, Miss Laurie, was Mariposa's music teacher; she fell in love with my son and talked him up to the director. Still, I couldn't get the school to return my phone calls.

I finally plopped Cole in the stroller one day, walked down the street, and rang the doorbell. Amazingly, the director, a woman with a reputation for being tough on parents, answered the door. She took one look at Cole and invited us in. We got a tour and were offered a place in the toddler class on the spot.

One month later, Cole was picking flowers and walking to school with his parents and grandparents in tow.

Cole's a lot like his dad and sisters: He does not love school. When I tell him in the morning that we have to turn off Noggin and get dressed, he moans, "Again!" Before he turned three, he started riding a small, red Radio Flyer bike with training wheels. I'd walk alongside, and Otis would run after. Cole would wait ten feet away down the sidewalk while I rang the school bell. When his teacher, Ms. Paola, a sweet, young Argentine whose colorful outfits I envied every morning, came to the gate, he would pedal up and make his grand entrance. I'd take off his helmet, hand him his backpack. "I have something to tell you," he said every morning. "I like you, and I love you, and I miss you." Then, he'd kiss and hug me and let Ms. Paola take him inside.

I'm not a Montessori nazi. If Mariposa weren't so close, maybe we would have gone somewhere else. We were fortunate that excellence was also convenient. There's a ton to be said for not having to throw a small child into a car seat every morning and drive through traffic in the name of his improvement. Plus, I get to walk home and have a couple hours alone to write. A happy mother makes for a happy child.

The first thing Cole learned was the names of all the animals. Then colors. Then yoga. At age three, he struggles to count to ten and is beginning to know his alphabet. More importantly, he's making friends. He and Dhillon, a solemn-faced, dark-haired boy, fight madly but want to be together every day. And then there's Audrey, a haunting, curly-haired, blue-eyed beauty whom Cole talks about constantly.

"You know what?" he asked me the other day. The most devilish smile captured his lips. "Audrey kissed me." Then, Cole laughed maniacally. "We're going to get married!" he shrieked, then went into his booty boogie, which looks a little like a chicken dance but entails rapping himself on the head and shouting, "Oh yeah, booty!" Like father, like son.

Cole has made me something I never thought I would be: baby crazy. Whereas I used to notice children only if they were crying, screaming, whining, or otherwise annoying me, now I watch them the way Bud watches attractive women. Dining al fresco at Miami Beach's Lincoln Road Mall, it's as if I'm at a tennis match, my head bobbing back and forth, following prams, battling Bug-a-boo envy. The kids see me looking, and I smile, as if we have a secret: "I have one of you!" my smile whispers.

My infant insanity is all the more surprising since I was such a perfect candidate for postpartum blues. I was ambivalent about parenting, had an already difficult household situation, enjoyed my work and overworked, and had a history of depression. I could so easily have lost it once I realized not only that I was not going to have time to write a book on maternity leave—like I had naively, incredibly thought I would—but that I wasn't going to be able to write a single chapter. Bringing up baby came naturally, but it was still a hell of a lot of work. Just as the Eskimos have a special word for the hardest, deepest, coldest snow, parents should come up with a term for that feeling they get after three months—or three years—of sleep deprivation. "Exhausted" only describes the tip of the iceberg.

I have moments, days even, of pure despondency, when I'm sure I'm not cut out for this parenting stuff. And I rage: at Bud, for being a typical, oblivious male; at the girls, for waking Cole up; at Cole, for biting his best friend on the back; at myself, for not controlling my temper. I worry I'm becoming everything I didn't want to be: a frumpy, grumpy housewife who, two weeks after it came out, still hasn't heard the new Strokes CD.

Then I remember: I don't like the Strokes.

14

Mamarama

❧   ❧   ❧

On October 10, 2003, I got an unusual e-mail at work:

Hi:

I read your article on Jacki-O, issued on October 6, 2003. In the article you mentioned that Poe Boy Entertainment—her record company—has an office in South Beach. Could you please supply me with the address? The reason I'm asking is that I collect intelligence on all current rappers and record companies in the South Beach area. Thank you for your co-operation in this matter.

The e-mail was signed by a Miami Beach Police Department (MBPD) detective. For years the New York Police Department (NYPD) had been rumored to have a hip-hop task force: officers charged with keeping an eye on an industry and genre that had become infamous for shootings. Undoubtedly aware they would be accused of racial profiling and other civil-liberties infractions, brass always denied the unit's existence. The "hip-hop cop" was an urban Sasquatch—often sighted but never confirmed. Now here, in black-and-white lettering on my computer screen, was an officer declaring that the city of Miami Beach was doing precisely what the NYPD denied.

I took the lead to Nicole White, a diligent, hip-hop-savvy *Herald* metro reporter who covered Miami Beach. I had written hundreds of CD reviews in my life, but I had never done an investigation like this. The story tapped into what I liked best about my job when I first came to the *Herald* after working for glossy New York magazines: being surrounded by colleagues who exposed corrupt union officials, political scandals, airport mismanagement, environmental screwups, and insurance fraud, rather than which celebrity was fucking which. I felt like Rocker Girl Friday, smart-talking her way through the cubicle maze of a big-city newspaper. The *Herald* gave me a hard-on for hard news.

Nicole and I had great chemistry. More than one colleague dubbed us the hip-hop Woodward and Bernstein: the political reporter and the counterculture aesthete, chasing down leads, bolstering background sources with on-the-record quotes, unearthing files. We, on the other hand, called ourselves the Supreme Team, a joking reference to Diana Ross's girl group and the crack cartel that allegedly financed one record label and its high-profile artists.

The detective's e-mail set off an extraordinary chain of events. Within a few months, officers had told us on the record that not only were there hip-hop cops on the beach and in Miami (two separate municipalities and police departments), but they had trained with departments from around the country at sessions in New York. In Miami's gang-unit office, Nicole and I paged through an inches-thick binder that the NYPD had compiled of rappers and their associates who had arrest records. There were mug shots, record company bios, articles, license plate numbers, and surveillance reports. We'd hit journalistic pay dirt.

"Police Secretly Watching Hip-Hop Artists" ran as the lead story in the *Miami Herald* on March 8, 2004. Just getting the story in was exhausting. Nicole and I had to carefully explain hip-hop culture and history to editors used to covering mayors and immigration. It was Winter Music Conference week, so I was working like mad, out late every night, interviewing DJs like Danger Mouse and Ben Watt. Thanks to the conference, when the story hit the stands, it found an instant audience of industry professionals. By the next day, it was international news.

Cole turned one year old two days after our scoop hit the stands. Thank Hera, Mom was in town to help. We put together a small party at a local park overlooking the Intracoastal Waterway. I didn't want an overblown bounce-house affair; I wasn't trying to impress anyone, just to enjoy a nice day, eat some good food, and surround my son with his favorite people. Mom pulled Cole and his friends around in a wagon, while boats zoomed by and I enjoyed a respite from the storm. In the middle of the celebration, a uniformed Miami Beach cop showed up. It was our friend and neighbor, an expectant dad himself, come for the party.

Children often are miserable at their own fiestas; it's their party, and they can cry if they want to. The excitement and pressure to have a good time can overwhelm. Plus, they have to share their toys. I'm happy to say Cole had a great time on the one-year anniversary of that maternity center miracle. No tears, no fights, little fussing.

It was a banner day for me, too, knowing I could be in the middle of the most intense experience of my journalistic career and still throw my son a good party.

Volumes have been written about how to "balance" career and family. I don't like that term. I am not a fulcrum. I prefer to see kids and jobs not as oppositional weights but as complementary pleasures. I want my life to be integrated, not pulled in different directions. Nor are work and family the only two interests—even the dominant interests—of us twenty-first-century foxes. Friendships, culture, politics, travel: We want the world, and we want it now, baby. I've never desired to be a wage slave any more than I wanted to be a housewife. I'm interested in creating this work-in-progress, my life, which involves writing, screwing, dining, dancing, protesting, sailing, and more.

During one of my many discussions with my friend Susie— punk rock photographer extraordinaire and mother of Eli—I decided we needed another word to describe the rock 'n' roll carnival ride our lives have become. An exclamation meant to convey the excitement and vertigo, the zest and dizziness, of our crammed days popped out of my mouth: mamarama!

It's a smooth-flowing word, a singular (and singing) state of being. But it has two parts. When our kids take over our lives, when we realize we haven't gotten out of the house in days, when we're not getting enough brain food or recreation or art, Susie and I say to each other, "Need more rama." It's a punning reference to the nonsense suffix adopted by at least two bands (Bananarama and Dramarama) and to a Hindu god (as in "Hare Rama"). I suppose there could be occasions when we would say, "Need more mama," but, somehow, those never come up.

Mamarama isn't about the perfect madness of trying to be an overachieving super mom; rather, it's about the idea that all moms are super. Just because we have kids doesn't mean we give up our diva glamour as culture mavens. In fact, parenting adds to our worldliness. Believe me, I'm much smarter now than I was B.C. (Before Cole), even if sometimes my thoughts are clouded by the sleep-deprived, multitasking exhaustion my mother superior friend and old college pal Janice calls "milk brain."

Mamarama is about changing the way we look at mothers, about realizing we are the cutting edge, the creators of the future. Check out a partial roll call of pop's great moms: Björk, Chrissie Hynde, Neneh Cherry, Madonna, Cyndi Lauper, Patti LaBelle, Gloria Estefan, Diana Ross, Patti Smith, Kristin Hersh, Ari Up, Liz Phair, Corin Tucker. One of the most transgressive acts I've ever seen on a stage was Hersh up there doing her mesmerized strum, her belly pushing out her guitar. "I understand blood, and I understand pain/There can be no life without them," the great Pretender Hynde rages on "I'm a Mother." Mamarama!

Our cops story touched a raw nerve in the racially divided polity of Miami. The city so fervently presents itself as international and cosmopolitan that many observers forget it's in the South. When I first moved here, I was stunned by the blatant racism that would come of out of the mouths of even supposedly cultured people. Sometimes the prejudice was veiled as anti-hip-hop; sometimes it wasn't veiled at all. As Joan Didion put it in her book *Miami*,

"Those gestures with which other troubled cities gradually learn to accommodate their citizens seemed not, in South Florida, to take hold."

Like ancient Greece, Miami is divided into city-states, many of them governed by tribes: Cubans in Hialeah, Jews in Miami Beach, WASPs in Coral Gables, blacks in Opalocka. As in apartheid-era South Africa, for decades you had to have a pass proving you were a citizen or worker to cross a causeway from the mainland to the beach. Blacks could work and star in beach hotels and clubs, but they couldn't spend the night, until Harry Belafonte busted that barrier in the '50s.

Long-simmering grievances erupted in a riot in 1980, when four cops were acquitted of beating to death Arthur McDuffie, an insurance agent and father who died in police custody. After exile politics led the city to snub Nelson Mandela in 1990 because he had met with Fidel Castro, black leaders organized a tourism and convention boycott of Miami that lasted three years.

By the time I moved to South Florida, this was all history—but recent history. African Americans were helping to make Miami a hot destination. Rap and R&B stars, along with athletes and other celebrities, were buying homes in South Florida and projecting voluptuous images of the city in videos. Hip-hop was bringing money, energy, and notoriety back to a region that, after the departure of Madonna, was just beginning to slip on the glam-o-meter.

On Memorial Day weekend 2001, hundreds of thousands of tourists converged on the beach for the celebrity-packed parties attached to what was supposed to be a small event, Urban Fashion Week. Taken by surprise by the sheer number of visitors, the city's resources were overwhelmed. Traffic stalled as women overflowed

their thongs and male admirers with camcorders recorded the pos-
teriors for posterity (or amateur porn sites). The streets were lit-
tered with promotional flyers, bottles, cans, coffee cups, condoms,
and fast-food containers. There were more than two hundred ar-
rests. The fact that most of the celebrants were black undoubtedly
shaped the tenor of the reaction to what some residents called an
"invasion."

It was after Memorial Day that beach cops went to New York to
bone up on the hip-hop culture that had taken the predominantly
white force by surprise. But far from enlightening them, the training seemed to have reinforced some officers' racist generalizations
about a genre that had long ago crossed color and economic barri-
ers to become the dominant sound of youth culture. Two officers
told Nicole and me that most rappers were criminals and/or gang
members. One showed us a list of rappers and their supposed gang
affiliations. Included on it were the suburban New Jersey group
Salt 'N' Pepa, a female outfit as likely to be affiliated with organized crime as Bon Jovi (then again, perhaps the latter should be
prosecuted for aural atrocities). At least the department had the
good sense to admit that Cheryl James, Sandy Denton, and
Pamela Greene (DJ Spinderella) were not known to be Crips or
Bloods.

The officers' comments showed why the news of a hip-hop task
force was so explosive. It stank of racial profiling and FBI COIN-
TELPRO tactics against civil rights activists, of the long-strained
relations between the black community and police. Of the Miami
Beach Police Department's 97 top officers, only 2 were African
American; Miami's police department had 26 out of 226. Of the
seventy-seven subjects in the binder, seventy-three were black.

Around the time our cops investigation hit the streets, there were a lot of things I'm sure Karlie wanted to call me, but Super Mom was not one of them. Bouncing from Michigan to New York to Miami, from grade school to junior high to high school, she was on her sixth school in as many years. The latest was an alternative program for potential dropouts. She'd wound up there after failing to show up for much of regular high school. Karlie has some sort of block or disability when it comes to math, but she's not stupid. A counselor diagnosed her with attention deficit disorder, manic depression, and a stressed-out, fucked-up life. Mostly, she was a troubled teen, under attack by hormones and horny guys. Bud, who ran away from home at fourteen to live with his brother and then dropped out of school, saw her behavior as normal, and even took a little pride in her antiauthoritarianism. He let her stay out all night, said nothing about the bottles of alcohol in her room, and mostly handled her with love and compassion, not discipline. It drove me crazy and scared me to death.

It's particularly easy to get into trouble in Babylon-by-the-bay Miami, to fall into a bad crowd, wind up on drugs, get pregnant, land in jail. Posses of boys followed gorgeous Karlie about; she rarely introduced them to us as they draped their bad attitudes over our couch. They were the gangsta-rap generation, modern-day rebels without a cause, enamored of thug role models (and oblivious to the more layered, thoughtful elocutions of underground hip-hop).

There's no ghetto in Miami Beach, I like to point out to the girls, though it's certainly not all lifestyles of the rich and famous either. These sullen children of hard-working immigrants and broken families, captivated by the American dream but not the American work ethic, were wannabe ghetto, trying to hustle their way into prosperity.

If I said anything about her choice of friends, her attitude, her problems, Karlie went ballistic. Angry and apprehensive, I was probably saying the wrong things. I was certainly an easy scapegoat for her many woes. I tried to stay out of it, to focus on Cole and work. But the angst of a fifteen-year-old girl whose body is growing through the roof is hard to contain in a (relatively) small house.

It's a conundrum: How does a mom who was a bit of a bad girl discipline her kids? What does the woman with three tattoos say when her teenage girls come home with fresh ink and piercings?

I was having sex and smoking pot in high school, wearing miniskirts, and saying fuck you to Ronald Reagan. But I was also getting straight A's. It wasn't so much what Karlie was doing that bothered me; it was what she wasn't doing: studying, working, creating . . . *anything*.

Unlike Bud, many parents I know who were the wildest youths are now the strictest disciplinarians. They know exactly what their children could be doing, and they won't let them stray a foot off the straight and narrow, even though they survived their own misdoings. Our neighbor Bill gave his military parents hell. Now he's a tugboat captain who curses like a sailor and makes sure his sweet, docile son and daughter do their homework every night. Vickie hasn't stopped partying since she was a teen, but she already talks about locking up her daughter when she reaches adolescence. I remember when I went to interview Patti Smith in her suburban Detroit turret. Her prepubescent daughter admired my purple hair streaks and asked her mom if she could get some. The punk matriarch said no. Maureen Tucker, drummer on such

Velvet Underground songs as "Heroin" and the S&M ode "Venus in Furs," once told me that she didn't let her kids watch MTV because it was too sexy.

There has to be a middle ground between strictness and permissiveness. I knew Bud and I hadn't found it.

My fear that Karlie's delinquency could harm the rest of us was realized one month after the hip-hop cops story broke. While we were on vacation in Puerto Rico, someone broke into our house. Among the items they stole was my *Herald* laptop—the one with the MBPD e-mail and other notes in its hard drive. Thousands of important documents and phone numbers were gone, in strangers' hands—not to mention that I now had to deal as a citizen with one of the police departments I had just investigated.

When I thought things couldn't get any worse, a local tabloid saw the police report and turned the break-in into a front-page story. The implication was that the crime was an inside job, a police cover-up, a conspiracy.

Maybe, I thought. It was certainly strange timing. But I believed a perhaps even more disturbing lead, that an associate of Karlie's, one of those would-be gangstas who had slouched on the couch, had made off with most of my jewelry.

That was Karlie's theory, too. There was a kid, call him Neal—no one liked him, she said—who heard we were going to be gone and talked big about busting in. The cops brought him in, and he confessed to the crime. But Neal said he hadn't acted alone: Leading the way, through the window that was hidden from sight and easy to open, was Dick, Karlie's best friend, a youth who, even after the break-in, had sat at our table and shared our supper.

The cops arrested both teens and recovered one ring and my computer. But the laptop had already been reprogrammed. I was angry and shaken. What if the thieves had broken in while we were home, while Cole was there? I hated fearing that we weren't safe in our own home.

Bad as the break-in was for me, for Karlie, it was the bottom that maybe she needed to hit. Her best friend had betrayed her, and she had endangered her family. From that point on, she cut herself off from the youths she had been hanging out with, stopped going out, pulled herself inside her shell and, eventually, back together again.

The dropout program saved her ass. Through night and summer school, she made up her lost credits. At seventeen, she graduated from Beach High with A's and B's—and a congratulatory (form) letter from President Bush.

I wish I could have reached her when she was in that dark place. I wish I hadn't said and done things that probably deepened the chasm between us. I think there are some things a parent can't fix; all you can do is stay on the ride and hope you come through the tunnel and out the other side.

Nicole and I unleashed a firestorm. Rock 'n' roll got waylaid by payola hearings, and the FBI had kept files on John Lennon, but never before had a genre of music been singled out for such explicit criminal surveillance. Within the week, Nicole and I were interviewed by reporters from England to Australia. We were also branded liars on national television by Miami's top cop, a red-faced Irish American named John Timoney.

The police departments all pointed fingers at each other. Miami alternately denied the binder's existence and promised to burn it, while the beach made the smoking gun public. A copy of the binder reportedly made its way to at least one South Beach club, where rappers scrambled to see if they were in it. Leaders of the American Civil Liberties Union and the Hip-Hop Summit Action Network, an organization founded by Russell Simmons, denounced the police. Community boards and panels convened hearings; at one unlikely public seminar, Timoney squared off against infamous dirty rapper Luther Campbell of 2 Live Crew and David Mays, controversial and outspoken publisher of the hip-hop magazine *The Source*.

Fellow journalists put our investigation through the wringer. Eventually, we were vindicated. Sgt. Derrick Parker, New York's original hip-hop cop, said in his 2006 memoir, *The Notorious C.O.P.*, that our piece blew his career out from under cover. Nicole and I won a few awards for our investigation. We've been featured in books and movies that make us look like underground heroes. It's much-needed satisfaction for a story that sometimes tore our lives apart.

Like any roller coaster ride, mamarama can be full of long, uphill climbs. It's hard to find the glamour in days of poo and spew. I don't have the time to put together a look like I used to; it's a constant battle against creeping frump. As Sarah, a newspaper editor and mother of three, said to me, "Some days it's all I can do to run a brush through my hair." I've fully capitulated to practical shoes. I try not to go to work with stains on my clothes, but some mornings, I forget to look in the mirror.

Fortunately, I have a sometimes glamourous job. Not long after "Police Secretly Watching Hip-Hop Artists" came out, MTV announced it was bringing the Video Music Awards (VMAs) to Miami in August. Nicole and I realized, and a MTV producer confirmed, that was one reason Miami officials flipped out over our story: They were in the middle of trying to snag the hottest show to yet hit this celebrity-obsessed burg. I can just see the sputtering civic leaders, so eager to pimp their city, sweating and offering excuses as an MTV exec slammed the *Herald* with our story down on a conference table.

The VMAs came to Miami two years in a row, saw their ratings drop each year, and were conquered by a hurricane and, irony of ironies, a hip-hop shooting. They were a silly, extravagant affair, nowhere near as much fun as the Art Basel Miami Beach art fair and Winter Music Conference; like so much culture in the aughties, they were more about image, too little about content. The famously talentless Paris Hilton was everywhere that first year, dancing on tables and trying to get into the tabloids. I didn't give a fuck about Paris Hilton (though I was pissed when I just missed OutKast's Andre 3000 at Mansion).

The VMAs did provide a few diva-mom moments.

The theme at '04's show was the upcoming election. MTV was trying to engineer the kind of full-court press that helped Clinton become president. The war in Iraq had led even the most self-and-bling-obsessed egos (i.e., P. Diddy) to get a political conscience. This time, however—typical of the narcissistic moral lethargy that defined the times—instead of uniting behind a cause, everyone seemed to look at the election as the chance to launch a brand: Vote for Change, Choose or Lose, Vote or Die. The day after the

VMAs, at a downtown Miami Foot Locker, Jay-Z unfurled his own banner, Voice Your Choice—along with his new sneaker line.

Jay-Z was up there with Michael, the Beatles, Bruce, Patti, and Lynn Breedlove in my pantheon of personal heroes. When Jay-Z brags, he's boosting all of us battling for self-esteem: "Ladies is pimps too, go on brush your shoulders off," Beyoncé's boo raps on *The Black Album*, one of the all-time great statements about show biz.

I had five minutes with the Marcy Projects drug-dealer turned midtown Manhattan mogul before Foot Locker let the autograph seekers in. Jay-Z laughed when I told him I was a fan. I guess he hadn't met many bespectacled, middle-aged, white women who had *Blueprint* on rotation in their CD players. But when I brought up the binder, in which he was featured, his tune changed.

"That was your story?" he said. "That was you? Man, you hit a home run with that. What do you reporters call it, when you get a story like that?"

"A scoop."

"A scoop. All right." And Jay-Z shook my hand.

Despite having narrowly missed Florida's four hurricanes in '04, the VMAs—gluttons for a drenching—came back the next year. This time they weren't as lucky; true to that year's water theme, Katrina drowned most of the events planned for VMA week. By Saturday, the rain was passing. I brought Kenda and her friends out to South Beach with me that afternoon, where hotels were hosting parties and tony product giveaways for all the visiting stars. She was amazed, star struck, giddy, snapping pictures on her cell phone of *OC* actors I'd never heard of.

Jay-Z was hanging out by the pool at the Loew's. He remembered me, shook my hand again, talked about the hurricane that hadn't yet decimated the Gulf Coast. I think I earned a free pass on several months of parenting transgressions when, oh so casually, I introduced Kenda to Mr. Carter. As a local DJ told her at the next party, "You have a cool-ass mom!"

Those were special occasions. The reality is that A.C. (After Cole), I don't get out like I used to. Nightlife and small children don't mix well; it's hard to stay out late when you have to get up early. There have been WMC nights when I've crawled into bed just as Cole is getting up, feeling fully decadent. Maybe if I worked the late shift all the time, I'd get used to it. I wish I could be like the chain-smoking heroines of the British sitcom *Absolutely Fabulous*, who don't let middle age or motherhood slow down their swinging London lifestyle.

I try. Every December, my music-junky girlfriends and I become Baselmaniacs. During the week when Art Basel Miami Beach brings thousands of galleries, artists, and collectors to South Florida, there's more great art than one could possibly take in without suffering a Stendhal-style overstimulation breakdown. There are also concerts, open bars, DJs, private parties at swank collectors' houses, hotel pool parties, condo rooftop parties, block parties, parties, parties, parties.

In 2004, I swore I was going to do Basel as I, pregnant and then nursing during the two previous years, hadn't done it before. Bud and Rosa were on notice that their services would be needed. I plotted the outfits I would wear.

But the best-laid plans of parental units often get shot to hell. That week, one of the kids brought me a present from school: lice. I could just picture myself at some waterfront mansion, maniacally scratching my scalp as I discoursed about Jeff Koons. Then, Cole got sick. Instead of checking out the installations in downtown warehouse spaces, I spent Friday night repeatedly getting covered with vomit.

Having a baby doesn't have to change everything, but it will surely reorder your priorities. Sometimes, I'm actually grateful that Miami has a lame live-music scene. When friends in normal cities tell me about all the bands coming through their town, I just shrug. I've seen plenty of concerts in my lifetime. If I added together all the hours I've spent standing around venues waiting for acts to come on, I'm sure I would figure I've wasted a year of my life holding a drink and looking bored. I took a long time rock 'n' rolling before I had Cole. I'm not wasting any more of it.

I admit, sometimes I get sick of watching *Finding Nemo* for the hundredth time or coming up with funny new character voices as I read *The Gruffalo* aloud. Then, Cole cuddles into me and sighs, "I love you too much." And I'm glad I'm not standing somewhere, staring at an empty stage, breathing in second-hand smoke, and wondering how much my lower back is going to hurt tomorrow.

Nicole and I never said the cops shouldn't be profiling rappers. We reported; we didn't editorialize. We knew well the danger surrounding some hip-hop artists; it was made clear early in the morning of the '05 VMAs, when a gunshot cleared the celebrity-packed Kanye West party at the elite Shore Club. I was getting ready to head over to the oceanfront hotel when I got the text message from

Nicole: "Suge shot." Suge Knight, the infamous head of Death Row (a.k.a. Da Row) Records, implicated by many in the assassinations of Tupac and Biggie, was a large part of the reason there were hip-hop cops in the first place. Now, he had a bullet in his ass.

Herald reporter Jackie Charles was in the club when the shots rang out. Nicole, reporter Audra Burch, photographer Joshua Prezant, and I were there within minutes. Finally, as I had fantasized decades ago, I was at the scene of a celebrity shooting. But like so many of my dreams and plans, this one didn't go as I'd pictured it. Maybe it was better, being a witness and a chronicler, not a fan and martyr.

The tenet of modern life I may have the hardest time with is carpe diem, living in the moment, acting like there's "No Day but To-day," as Jon Larson wrote in *Rent*. I'm such a dreamer, always thinking about tomorrow, making plans, analyzing, writing the story of what happens as it happens, living in my head. As Bud says, I "brain-work" things to death. Sometimes I feel sorry for Cole, having such an absentminded mom. "You're not listening!" he says when I lose the thread of one of his winding tales and answer him with, "Huh?" That's why he loves Papa so much: My dad moves at his pace, stopping to smell the roses, not forever pulling him along.

This part of me, my son has changed: Cole pulls my head out of the clouds and puts my feet back on earth. Every day he reminds me to be present, to stop thinking about work, or what has to be done around the house, or the book I'm reading, or the singer I'm obsessing about. Never mind the destination; mama-rama is all about the ride.

15

About a Boy (and Girls)

Ꝋ Ꝋ Ꝋ

Let me tell you about my son. A Florida baby, Cole's got coloring to die for: curls bleached golden year-round, deep brown eyes, skin a healthy tan. Girls would kill for his long lashes. Luscious, luscious lips and his dad's round cheeks give him a cherubic, mischievous face. His little nose comes from me, I think. People say he looks like us; I see the faces of his uncles Brett and Bob in Cole's little mug. He is short, like his parents; has a bit of a tummy (like us). Like his sisters, he's definitely a looker. I'm sure most parents think their baby's a babe. I know ours is.

Cole has a killer memory. If you tell him today you're going to do something tomorrow, you can be sure he won't forget. Like most kids, he's not a big fan of having his hair cut. "But your bangs are over your eyes!" we told him once, as we forced him to the barber. A few months later, when we tried to take him back, he looked at us as if we were idiots: "It's not touching my eyes," he said, pointing to his brow.

Cole was slow to talk and is making up for lost time. He launches into these long spiels about the day's activities: "I'm going to catch a little fish, and then I'm going to catch a big fish, and then I'm going to take them home to mama, and then she's going to cook them, and then we're going to eat them and say, 'yum!' and be happy!" Cole's stories usually have happy endings. I don't think that's Disney's influence; I think it's the natural wish of a child. The language we call "Colish" involves frequent doubling of words: "I told told you so!" "I no no wipe my bum bum." It includes sprinklings of *Español*, which I fail to recognize, until Rosa tells me "idy" is his version of *ardilla*, Spanish for "squirrel."

Cole's still adept at the backbend he was born doing. He's always throwing his head back, in laughter or a tantrum. He has his dad's and sisters' athleticism, was walking at nine months, swimming at twelve months, dribbling a soccer ball at two years, breakdancing at two and a half. A propos of nothing, he likes to go into downward-facing dog, which he's learned in yoga class at school. When he does something good or cool—speak Spanish, or catch a ball—he executes this joyous victory dance: kicking his legs, side-stepping, punching his fists, clapping his hands, chanting, "Oh yeah!" He likes to dance. Kenda's boyfriend, Abraham, is teaching him b-boy moves, to spin on the ground like a top. That's not to be confused with the Worm, which apparently Cole has also learned. He'll show you the difference, if you get it wrong, going from a roll—"That's not break-dancing"—to a windmill—"this is break-dancing!" My son's a bilingual b-boy; how Miami is that?

"He's such a boy," people say, when they see him tearing up the sidewalk on his bike or shooting everything in sight with a stick. He's obsessed with boyhood, too: with killing "bad boys," with being a "good boy," with cowboys and b-boys. When a playdate with a male friend inevitably involves some shoving establishment of boundaries, when he stares google-eyed at Angelina Jolie's sexy character in *Shark Tale*, when a cheap plastic sword supplants all his wooden toys and soft animals as his favorite fetish object, I have to wonder: How much behavior is hardwired at the hormonal level? If a lot, does that mean tomboy me had an excess of testosterone? Were Brett and I abnormal because I got into more fights than he did? Doesn't saying, "That's so boy," encourage Cole to behave a certain way? Do Power Rangers promote his midget machismo, just like Barbies indoctrinate girls with femininity?

Raising a male in the twenty-first century is a challenge—and a chance—for a feminist. Sometimes I can't get my son to stop pounding on me with his fists or shooting everything in sight with his plastic pistol. (One time, he walked up to a statue at a Chinese restaurant and shot Buddha's big belly. Quite un-Zen.) At those moments, I wonder if the brother really is from another planet: if not Mars, then Pluto. Then, I watch Cole's girlfriends and my friends' daughters fuss over their pink plastic vanity sets or dissolve into giggling puddles over some nonsense, and I think that maybe I have more in common with Cole after all.

I feel sorry for girls now, who are growing up not, as I did, in the sunlight of feminism but in the shadows of the neocon backlash. I don't see them dreaming about becoming president. I see them obsessed with their current status as princesses. I hear them singing not Joan Jett's "Bad Reputation" but "Cater 2 U," as they mimic the perfectly manicured bell tones and gestures of Destiny's Child. (The all-girl vocal group's career trajectory vividly illustrates feminist backsliding, from "Independent Women," to rapper arm jewelry, to oblivion.)

I call it the Princess Tyranny (PT). Visit the girls' department of any store, and you'll suffer cutesy overkill: T-shirts that say "princess" with little pink crowns dotting the "i." Wands. Tutus. Ballet shoes. The Princess line of Barbie (talk about a double negative). Even teenagers' clothes proudly declare their wearers wannabe Snow Whites, Sleeping Beauties, or, puh-lease, Daddy's Little Girl. The other day, I saw a sunshade in the window of an SUV that said "The Princess Is Out" in pink and leopard print. That princess was old enough to drive.

"Girls just want it to be their birthday every day," my friend Cathay says, defending the PT. It's true: Princess parties are to the aughties what horse-riding parties were to the '70s. Gone are the sweet, simple, little sadistic affairs of Norman Rockwell past, like Pin the Tail on the Donkey and piñata bashing. The toddler blowouts of the twenty-first century entail small staffs and cause annual temporary bankruptcies. They are all about parents showing that they are the best parents, about proving that they love their kids the most by showering them with the greatest number of party favors, bounce houses, pizzas, clowns, face painters, ponies, sing-alongs, games, mermaids, and walking Barneys. Not to mention cake.

Unfortunately, on the second birthday of Cole's sweet little classmate Violet, it rained like hell. (As I like to say about Florida on those days when the water runs up the storm drains, not down them: Sunshine State my ass.) I can't imagine what kind of production her parents had planned for their Bay Road estate. I just know they didn't want kids tracking mud on the carpet. So, the rug rats and their entourages were rerouted to the penthouse of South Beach's chichi Raleigh Hotel, where it cost $15 for a valet to park

our car. I had to ask Kenda to make sure she had gotten the address right when she took the message: Yes, the top floor of the
swank resort owned by Uma Thurman's then boyfriend, Andre
Balasz; the party space with eighth-floor views of the Atlantic that
car companies rent out for twenty grand in order to sway tastemakers with trendy DJs, free drinks, and hired models/hookers. That's
where Cole, Violet, and the rest of the Montessori munchkins
went to spit up strawberries and throw grapes.

Who knows what outdoor fun was left melting on Bay Road,
what deposits for toy castles and inflatable dragons were lost. The
woman hired to dress as Cinderella and her young Tinkerbell assistant did make the move to SoBe. If your child didn't come
dressed up, they provided costumes that would transform him or
her into Snow White, Belle, or Prince Charming. They sprinkled
the girls' hair with fairy dust, then handed them wands and
crowns. The poor little things, having only learned to walk a year
ago, struggled to maneuver in plastic pumps around the expensive
furniture.

Kick off your shoes and run, I wanted to say. Run fast and far,
for that Cinderella is really the Wicked Witch, wanting to sap your
courage, your strength, your very ability to stand on your own two
feet.

Cole was happy, once he woke up and got a sword in his hand.
As he lay on the couch for the first hour, I joked that he had come
as Sleeping Beauty.

With their squished noses and puffy cheeks, the children were
all beautiful and precious. But in the bodies of their parents, good
people overflowing with love and generosity for their offspring, I
mourned the disappearance of distinction. I live in a city where a

disturbing number of otherwise seemingly sane people want to look like Ken and Barbie. It was a room full of impossible cheekbones, idealized eyebrows, cantilevered breasts, Popeye deltoids.

A photographer who looked like a model followed Violet around, diving in front of other children and on top of parents to catch her every blink. When her classmate Emily was crying after having bashed herself with her own wand, Violet walked up, patted her sweetly, and asked, "Are you okay?"

When I was a kid, princesses were not cool. They were pampered and spoiled and too fragile to be fun. Tomboys like Scout in *To Kill a Mockingbird*, Jo in *Little Women*, or Tatum O'Neal's character in *Paper Moon* were the preferred ideal. We weren't denying our femaleness, just the feminine mystique. We wanted to be heroines who could run and kick a soccer ball.

There are role models like that now. I mean, I wish I had had a Mia Hamm, Dora the Explorer, Venus and Serena Williams, or Teresa Weatherspoon to look up to. However, I don't see those women's pictures on Cole's friends' walls. Maybe it's because I live in heavily Hispanic Miami, where immigrants lured by the American dream tend to have more traditional social views, but I see Jessica Simpson, the Little Mermaid, and Christina Aguilera—hyperfeminine, ultrathin, pretty, girlie-girl icons.

From Shirley Temple to JonBenet Ramsey, we have not come a long way baby.

Reclamation of girl culture was part of the early '90s agenda for which my friends and I fought hard. That era's punk-inspired feminists called themselves Riot Grrrls, after all, not women. Three college-age friends from Olympia, Washington, and Washington,

D.C., gave their band the regressive moniker Bratmobile. They recorded an album, *Pottymouth*, whose artwork included pictures of them as tykes, as did many Riot Grrrl recordings. It was as if everyone was nostalgic for an earlier age, before puberty and Reagan hit. Singer Allison Wolfe leapt about on stage and shouted such anthems as "Cool Schmool" and "Kiss & Ride" like a hyperactive cheerleader. Meanwhile, Bikini Kill celebrated the "Rebel Girl" who drove "the coolest trike in town" (and who was "the coolest dyke"). It was a revolution, girl style, and a revolution in girl style.

When Bratmobile weren't sticking their tongues out, they had them lodged firmly in cheek. They weren't just girls, they were grrrls, a joking takeoff on '70s separatists' "womyn." And they were bad girls, not in a Britney Spears, jailbait-tease, fuck-me kind of way, but in an outspoken, shit-talking, fuck-you way. They weren't celebrating infantilism: They were imploding it.

So, how did we go from "girls kick ass" to "princesses rule"? Where did the left turn become a right? It turns out good old German philosopher Georg Wilhelm Friedrich Hegel was only half-correct. Culture can take two steps forward, one back, yes. But it can also take one step forward, drop the ball, turn around, punt the ball, and run like hell.

Rewind: When Riot Grrrl slogans began bubbling up from underground, the media lapped them up like so many pedophilic pundits. The subcultural uprising coincided with the pop-psych phenom of *Reviving Ophelia*. Suddenly, everyone was talking about girls. Instead of pushing their advantage, the freaked-out OGs (original grrrls) retreated, calling for a ban on talking to journalists, burrowing deeper underground, descending into infighting.

They left the revolution in hands that were, at best, misunderstanding and, at worst, sinister. One English bloke, no doubt having seen "Revolution Girl Style" on the covers of his country's music tabloids and sensing the gaping hole left by the grrrls, found five females with more modeling than musical profiles, gave them each silly names, and collectively called them the Spice Girls. He pronounced the hackneyed appropriation Girl Power. From there the backsliding accelerated, through the teen queens and Bratz dolls, culminating in the Princess Tyranny. By 2004, the grrr had gone out of girl culture.

Princesses may be cute, but they are helpless. They are easily duped by smarter, albeit evil, people (usually bad-ass spinster witches). Princesses have to be rescued, by men, of course. That gets boring real quick.

Still, I can see feminist traces in little girls carving out identities and images that are distinctly their own, free of icky boys. Princesses have a certain power, objectified, temporary, and patronized as it may be. As I watch them dress up like dolls and pretend to pour each other tea, I wonder, are they just miniature versions of Carrie Bradshaw and friends in *Sex and the City*? Are independent, child-free, professional women the true keepers of the Princess Tyranny? Am I, in fact, jealous?

There is one thing parenting does change, would-be mommies: You are no longer the princess. Your tutu will get torn. The thing you love most in the world will take your crown and place it on her head. And you will have to graciously, happily, lovingly surrender the throne, the spotlight, the center of attention to your child.

For some of my female friends who have not had children, I can see that abdicating this throne may be the biggest challenge of all. It was a lesson I, too, fought ferociously for years as my stepdaughters and I all sought their father's interest. (My bad, girls.) I remember Jane, a friend of mine who wants very much to have a child, playing Monopoly with Nadia, the eleven-year-old friend of my stepdaughter. Jane was so keen to win the stupid game, she tried to convince Nadia to trade Baltic for Broadway. It made me wonder: If Jane has a girl, will she learn not to compete with her? Or will she be unable to lose her identity as the winner, the best?

Leaving your princess throne, painfully humbling as it can be, is one of parenting's biggest rewards. You get to (have to) grow up. But don't worry: You may lose your princess crown to mommyhood, but your power only increases. On your head a new mantle descends: You are now the queen.

Queens are where it's at. Elizabeth I, Cleopatra, Latifah: What princess has affected history the way those dames have? Queens, literally, rule. As a monarch, you get to make decisions that affect the whole nation-state of your family. You don't have to wait for some guy to come along and kiss you to life.

We knew this, back in the '90s. Our leaders didn't sing of princesses. "You are the queen of my world," Kathleen Hanna crooned to her "Rebel Girl." Wronged English country lass Polly Jean Harvey sang of an avenging "50 Foot Queenie": "Tell you my name, F-U-C-K." The last song on *Pottymouth*? A bit of romantic boasting called "Queenie." And in the '70s, seminal grrrl rockers the Runaways declared themselves "Queens of Noise" (a title mamas surely can relate to).

Our culture may have regressed to a medieval fantasy of delicate, ornamental girls languishing until they are saved by square-jawed Republicans. But as a queen, you don't have to wait for some boy to rescue you. You can issue the order yourself.

A few months after Violet's birthday bash, there was yet another princess party. This one was at the Miami Children's Museum, a more suitable, if less royal, location than the Raleigh. As soon as we got there, Cole dutifully picked up one of the plastic swords, shields, breastplates, and helmets that were lying about, suited up, and promptly began dueling with Bill. Bill was all aggressive, wild swinging, but Cole was like a ballet dancer, waiting for an opening, leaping in and out, using his shield; it turned out that Mom, who was visiting, had been fencing with him all week. A couple other little boys tried to join in. But it was Violet who showed the truest fighting spirit, matching Cole's and Bill's thrusts and parries with a steely resolve and fierce expression. Other parents looked disgusted with the wanton display of toddler violence, but Violet's dad, in the corner coaching her, beamed at the glorious bitch his princess had become.

Where everyone around me sees the destiny of biology, I still see the influence of environment. Trucks were early favorite toys of Cole. So were dolls. I bought him both. But if my friend's Cuban grandmother sees her grandson playing with a doll, she freaks out. Now Aidan's a car freak, and his sister Laila loves princesses. That was not just genetics.

Put a toy sword in front of a kid, and she'll swing it. Everyone wants a taste of phallic power.

Sometimes I worry that my son, born in Armageddon times, is growing up to be a warrior. Other times, I hope he is. Bud has watched Westerns and war movies with Cole since he was a baby.

As a hater of guns and violence, I've had to swallow my tongue not to stop it: Bud has a right to raise his child too. Cole needs a role model to help him navigate the tricky waters of masculinity. They get something from those shows—a sense of honor, excitement, pride, and integrity—that I find corny but also respect. Given the times we live in, Cole probably needs to understand man's seeming instinct—or at least inclination—to fight. Hopefully, we'll raise him to value the more important goal of peace. For now, it's clear to me that he was not born with a trigger finger but got it from TV.

To balance the pulls of socialization, because I think the world has plenty of warriors, Cole and I watch *Snow White* and *Sleeping Beauty*. He loves those fairy tale romances. I've loaded his room with cute and cuddly stuffed animals. He prefers the more realistic, plastic ones, but at least they're a distraction from the few weapons he owns.

My son is not an easy child. He whines, cries, fusses, won't listen, throws fits, hurls toys, kicks, hits, and bites. That woman at Target who's hissing at her tantruming son, the evil mom with the evil child whom I said I would never become? That's been me. When I'm at a party with all those hippie-chick parents who don't let their kids watch TV or have guns, I'm on pins and needles, praying Cole won't kick a kid to the ground and start shooting him. I'm sure I make things worse when I jump on him for merely rubbing against some little boy's shoulder. I'm no better than he is: I don't believe in corporal punishment, but I've spanked him more than once in frustration.

Cole is a mama's boy. I've spoiled my son, let him become a whiner and crybaby because every time he simpers, I react. I've propagated "momism" in Philip Wylie's original, horrifically misogynist definition of the word: excessive mothering. I've doted on Cole because he's this great gift that I got when I least expected it, and I feel I must experience the hell out of him—when I'm not working. I've touched him too much; he's way too physical. He reacts to frustration with fists and tears; he's obsessed with my goddamned armpit.

In short, I know with dread certainty that my son will become a sociopath. All the signs are there: oral fixation, mama's boy, loves gunplay, short fuse, can't cope with frustrations. He will live with me, like David Souter, until he's a grown man, then he will attack screaming blondes while they innocently shower. I'm preparing myself for the day I will mouth, "I love you" to my biter as the bailiffs lead him out of the courthouse to his life imprisonment.

Or maybe not. Maybe these are the guilty ramblings of a middle-class, middle-aged, middle-American, working mom with sometimes gothic tendencies.

When he's a good boy, Cole's very very good. He loves to make people laugh. He's got a Chaplinesque sense of physical comedy and is turning into a storyteller. He likes to "shake his booty!" (that Miami influence again). The little blond boy in *Meet the Fockers*? The titular monkey in the film *Curious George*? That's Cole.

The truth of the matter is, Cole's received more bites and punches from his precious little Montessori classmates than he's dealt. He prefers playing with girls over boys. Every time I sneak by the school and spy on him at recess, he's sitting on a teeter-totter with two little girls, shouting, "Up, down! Up, down!"

One day when Cole was two, we were at a friend's house for dinner. It was the first day he figured out how to channel surf. He grabbed the strange remote control, which I hadn't even figured out how to operate yet, and flicked past a football game, hyperkinetic cartoons, Animal Planet, a romantic comedy, *That '70s Show*, looking for something to keep him entertained while the host's children slept and the boring parents talked.

Suddenly, he stopped. A woman was singing on the plasma screen. She looked a little like his "abba," short for *abuela*, the Spanish word for "grandmother," the name he calls my mother. She sounded like Abba, too, like maybe Cole, somewhere in his being, remembers my mom crooning to him in his little tub, when he was just a few days old. Judy Garland is one of her favorites, after all: a talented, tragic singer, actress, and mother. Maybe Cole was making the connection, recognizing the hairstyle of a vintage era and the trilling projection of a theatrically trained vocalist.

Or maybe he was just responding to beautiful music, a stylish lady, a sad song. It was certainly an odd choice for a scrappy little toddler boy: an old black-and-white PBS special with no Technicolor special effects, pop-up graphics, killer robots, or anthropomorphic dinosaurs. Maybe Cole was rivited because the Judy Garland special was different, an island of sanity amid the hyperactivity.

Though he can be fussy and a neatnik, I know Cole will never be a princess. That day, however, watching him fixate on a gay icon of another era, thinking how proud my mother and brothers would be, I thought, Maybe there's a queen in there.

Worse than watching Westerns with him, Bud listens to classic rock with Cole. "Wemember my song?" my son will ask. And then he starts singing, "We will, we will, wock you!" Queen again.

He'll program a song on the keyboard and say, "You know what that is? That's rock 'n' roll! That's my favorite!"

"What about hip-hop?" I ask.

Cole thinks about it. "I like hip-hop. But it makes me loud."

Art seems to be his favorite hobby, something he gets from his dad, not the mama with lousy hand-eye coordination. Bud can make the cutest little animals out of clay or build a nest and put a bird and eggs in it. Me, I draw the same old simple line figures over and over: bunny, flower, cat, sun. Cole paints, draws, or plays with clay almost everyday. The things he makes don't look like anything yet, to others at least. But I can tell Cole sees the world in his creations.

Cole's father and I like to joke that hopefully he'll get my brain smarts and Bud's body skills—and not the other way around. I think that's happening. He amazes me sometimes, the things he says at three years old. The other day we had a big hug. He sighed and said, "Do you know where I feel that? I feel that in my heart," and my son put his hand on his chest.

Maybe he'll revive the tradition of the gentleman soldier and scholar: the cultured, wise, brave intellectual who only resorts to violence as a last defense of honor and family. At least, that's what I think Bud's hero Clint Eastwood does.

I admit, I've become Cole-dependent. It's not the unconditional love I receive but that which I give that has been parenting's great gift to my middle years. Just listening to my son sigh in his sleep, I hear a symphony—he brings such joy to me. Sometimes I try to picture him at five, at eight, at twelve, at sixteen, as a young man, going off to college or to work or to see the world. It's an incredible thought, something I never imagined in all my wildest dreams: that I would watch my child grow up.

16

Dig the New Breeders

Oo   Oo   Oo

At thirty-eight years old, I faced not merely the birth of a new life but the death of a particularly prolonged adolescence. At least I wasn't alone. As a middle-aged mama in 2003, my rebel soul found itself riding two demographic trends. One, I was adding my drop to the bucket of the post–9/11 population explosion. For reasons that historians and scientists will probably spend years analyzing—the inevitable result of nights spent clutching each other for support? A cosmic desire to replace all those incinerated lives? Some scary biological drive to build armies? A collective "fuck-you Osama Bin Laden" fuck?—a lot of couples responded to terror with love. I had grown up in the shadow of one baby boom; now I was helping spawn another.

Two, I was part of the rising tide of mommy-come-latelies. Many women of my generation waited, and waited, and waited to procreate. We built careers, made hit records, wrote books. We figured out who we were before we decided to make another of us. At Cole's school, and among my circle of friends, parents in their mid-thirties and older are the norm. (That's probably why so many of his classmates are twins, the frequent fruit of fertility treatments.)

Together, these trends have made me a sometimes unwilling participant in what's been called "the new momism." Babies are the accessories of the aughties. Everyone is having them, from Britney Spears to Angelina Jolie to fifty-year-old could-be grandmas. It's trendy; it's cool; it's patriotic! And it can be sickening.

Authors Susan Douglas and Meredith Michaels have called the retro notion that parenting is the key to women's fulfillment "The Mommy Myth." It's an insidious ideology, especially as it serves a fundamentalist agenda that disguises itself as pro-family but is really pro-hate. The Mommy Myth takes women back to the '50s, when they quit their wartime jobs en masse to devote themselves to polishing the appliance-laden kitchen. I watch mothers now, painstakingly following Martha Stewart's hors d'ouevre recipes and dust-busting the minivan, and want to take their hands, lead them out to the street, hand them a copy of Judith Warner's book *Perfect Madness: Motherhood in the Age of Anxiety* and Sleater-Kinney's CD *The Woods*, and tell them not to answer their cell phones until we have a national, paid maternity-leave program and federally funded day care for all.

To comprehend and dispel the spell of familyphilia, take the teen-pop stars—please.

First, Britney, Jessica, and Christina et al. turned back the clock of feminist progress by acting like Lolitas while preaching virginity. Then, they ran around getting married and, in Britney's case, having kids at an age when it might have been more productive if they had realized their careers were over and they had better start thinking about Plan B (life as has-beens). It's scarcely a surprise that as quickly as she was a newlywed, the living doll Jessica Simpson was newly divorced. Watching starlets' train-wreck lives, it's as if women's lib never happened. Their crashes reinforce precisely how much feminism is needed, why Britney should have gotten some self-esteem from learning to play an instrument or producing a record, not inflating her tits. Thirty years ago, even a tragically vulnerable star like Karen Carpenter played drums.

The pop tarts have become perfect role models for what not to be—if little girls haven't already been so brainwashed that they can't see past the dying flashbulbs of fame.

I continue to believe that women shouldn't have to have kids to feel successful or complete. I give daily thanks to the activist pioneers who made the lifestyle choice of independence possible for me and my peers. I'm glad I finally found my way to mommyhood, but I probably could have had an equally fabulous (albeit socially less acceptable) life as a globe-trotting, bisexual, bachelorette novelist. I would never rank one lifestyle above the other.

Still, sometimes I jokingly call myself a born-again breeder, a momist, if you will. The pendulum of feminist self-determination shouldn't swing so far the other way: We shouldn't have to not have kids to feel like successful women.

A few months after I met Bud and his daughters, I went to interview my old Throwing Muses pal Kristin Hersh at her home near Joshua Tree, California, for *Request* magazine. She lived with her husband and manager Billy, her seven-year-old son Ryder, and her eleven-month-old Wyatt in a beautiful wood-beamed and tin-roofed retreat in a surreal high-desert landscape she described as "white-trash moon." Our lives had followed similar trajectories in the decade since we had first met: We had both battled depression as young women, left Rhode Island, made our fortunes following our, er, muses, and survived the public breakup of our greatest artistic collaboration. Throwing Muses' 1986 debut was a hit in England. The band was one of the first "alternative rock" groups, and certainly one of the first female-led ones, to get signed to a major U.S. label in the mid '80s—and to the same label as Madonna, no less. But the Muses never had the success of their friends R.E.M. or an Alanis Morrissette, maybe because Hersh never learned to write Top 40 anthems or peddle pop psychosis.

Unlike me, beginning shortly after our initial interview in Providence, Kristin had had children. She lost custody of her first, Dylan, in part because of her unconventional work schedule and her delicate mental health (at eighteen, she was diagnosed as schizophrenic). When I caught up with her again a decade later, she was still mourning—and fighting—that separation.

Kristin was releasing her first solo album since the band broke up. She'd recorded *Strange Angels* a year earlier. Since then, she hadn't listened to the album or written any new songs, she told me as she sat on a balcony with a stunning view of the desert, Wyatt sucking nourishment from her breast. She said the strange angels who had given her voice all these years had disappeared, and she didn't care if they never came back; she was happy being a full-time mother.

"I'm raising kids all day. That's my work," she said. "It's like climbing a mountain every day. And it's a good mountain and a physical one, and you're high off it. And then I go to work and have to hear again, 'There's too many female singer/songwriters on the radio,' et cetera. And nobody says, 'There's too many female mothers; you can't bring your kids to the pediatrician this week.' [Motherhood] actually works in the world. It's effective."

I was dismayed at the idea of another strong female icon subsuming her voice to her children. But I was also sympathetic to her feeling that parenting was more rewarding than being a singer/songwriter in the era of the Spice Girls.

Hersh's muses came back. She released two albums in 2005, one with the re-formed Throwing Muses. Maybe far from distracting her, parenting gave her self-esteem the boost it needed, reaffirmed her internal strengths rather than forcing her to rely on external approval—the male gaze (and the male ear). Patti Smith came back from Detroit and the '80s too. Cole helped me comprehend my heroines' absences, the selfish demands of nesting, especially during kids' first years, when they are so fragile and needy. I learned that motherhood is not the change in life I had feared; it's a new chapter, or two. Maybe a book.

It's a telling indicator of cultural misogyny that the varying meanings of "momism," a domineering matriarchy or excessive heteronormativity, have always been negative.

I'd like to reclaim momism as a growing branch of activism. The "motherhood movement," as one book dubs this outgrowth of feminism, could be to the aughties what civil rights were to the '60s. The first person to become a real, galvanizing leader of protest against war in Iraq was a mother who lost her son there: Cindy Sheehan. The United States could be about to have its first mom president. Mothers bear the greatest burden of an educational system that values testing over raising teacher salaries and reducing class sizes. Don't be surprised if rage at a government that can spend millions to bring "democracy" to foreign countries but can't guarantee its own people paid parental leave, subsidized child care, or universal health care spills out on the streets—or inspires a bedroom act along the lines of Lysistrata's. Our numbers are certainly strong; hear us roar.

I'm talking about a mother's revolution, but I'm not necessarily talking about our mothers' revolution, though I'm not discounting the importance of the groundwork they laid. A new breed of breeders is emerging, with their own magazines, books, rock bands, websites, and agendas. A single mother in her thirties in California spawned us. Anne Lamott's 1993 *Operating Instructions: A Journal of My Son's First Year* is the mother of all momoirs, revealing in intimate detail how it is possible to be a bohemian artist, recovering alcoholic, churchgoer, impoverished provider, and doting parent. Another single mom, Ariel Gore, gave us tattooed love parents a name: *Hipmama*, she called her fanzine, which became the basis for a series of books. Now, magazines like *Brain, Child* offer alternatives to the usual parenting glossies for us moms who are looking for more than holiday cookie recipes or craft ideas, who are more interested in the new They Might Be Giants CD than the Wiggles.

Call us M.W.A., mothers with attitude.

Once again, the personal is political. As in every stage of my life, I've found great comfort in womankind. Other mothers have helped me figure out how to manage my load when it seemed impossible, assured me that Cole and I are normal—or, if it's what I needed to hear, abnormal. They're my new sorority, and many of them are my old sisters, longtime friends such as Cindy, Kathy, and Vickie. We don't represent the nuclear family dream—more like the aftermath of the meltdown. Some of our parent-and-child constructions have two mommies, some only one and no daddy. Some of us adopted. Some of us grafted broken families, creating new species. All of us are everyday heroines.

Debbi had Blake nine months before I had Cole. That made me a perfectly timed recipient not only of maternity clothes, bedding, onesies, and a stroller, but more importantly of just-been-there advice. Debbi has the practical, progressive frontier spirit of New Zealand women; hers was the steady voice of reason I needed when I panicked over nursing, crying jags, and flying with a baby ("We just put him on a blanket under our feet and he slept the whole way," she e-mailed me). Her can-do-it-yourself-ism sadly came in handy when she realized her husband was hiding a cocaine and alcohol addiction and the task of caring for Blake fell on her competent but shaken shoulders.

Susie's husband, Harry, is paralyzed. They tried for years but weren't able to reproduce, so they adopted Eli from a teenage Native American couple. Both sets of parents flew to Hawaii (where there are progressive adoption laws) for the birth. Susie and Harry were there at the hospital with flowers for the couple that was handing them the gift of life. In their backyard, they've built Eli a wonderland: a pool with a waterfall, a tree house with a thatched Chickee-hut roof, a wooden playground. They are my role models of loving, supportive, slightly kooky parents.

When Eli was a baby and I was child free, I used to worry that Susie, whose photos of 1980s D.C. punk helped define the black-and-white hardcore aesthetic, was losing her rebel soul to her demanding son. I could never get her to go out; her days were structured around nap time. Then, Cole came along. I learned to say to Bud, as I watched Susie struggling to control a tantruming toddler, "There's the future"—and to know, as Eli turns into a gifted, curly-haired beauty and a caring big-brother figure to Colie, that that's a good thing.

Laura and her husband, James, raised three kids while simultaneously running one of the world's coolest concert agencies. I've watched Laura cart her kids to soccer games and bar mitzvahs in between producing shows by such international acts as Ojos de Brujo, Caetano Veloso, Nouvelle Vague, and the Brazilian Girls. James Junior, Christina, and Patrick help her stick flyers in stores and sell soda and CDs at shows. No stay-at-home mom, Laura's always up for going out, even at 11 p.m. Once, at a concert by sexy goth synth band the Faint, we looked around the room and realized we were surrounded by kids who could well be her son's and my daughters' classmates. We giggled, shrugged, and kept dancing. Those kids can only hope one day to be the cool-ass mothers we are.

Laila is Cole's first girlfriend. She's two years older and lives three doors down. Cole's actually closer in age to her brother, Aidan, but he usually only has eyes for Laila. Lili is one of those moms that never stops, running from swim class to piano lesson to birthday party, all while working full-time as a graphic designer. Her children have spent long days at day care since they were very young and seem perfectly fine, albeit as willful as Cole. One day, their father and I were watching them run around the local farmer's market, screaming and banging into people. Joseph looked at me and said, "We have wild kids, don't we?"

But then, coming back from dinner at the local pizza parlor one night, Laila climbed into the red Radio Flyer wagon, and

Cole leaned back into her arms. Bud pulled the little lovers home. Who needs sisters when you have neighbors?

Once a month, I meet with about ten other women for dinner and discussion of that month's reading. But since all but one of the book-club members have small children, the conversation inevitably turns from *The Kite Runner* or *Sarah* to our babies' bedtimes, summer camp, or our sex lives. Even if we haven't read the book, we'll drop almost anything for our scheduled rendezvous; "I NEED BOOK CLUB" is a refrain of our group e-mails.

A few of us have revived my old all-girl listening parties; now, we meet to make mixed CDs, not mixed tapes. One month, Jordan Levin, the Latin music critic for the *Herald* (yes, the paper has two women music critics), brought a track by the Colombian singer Andrea Echeverri. A few years older than me, Jordan blazed her way through the East Village and South Beach as a dancer and performance artist. She gave birth naturally at age forty-three at the same birth center as I had and is as crazy about Romina as I am about Cole. On "Lactochampeta," Echeverri sings in Spanish about the erotic joy of nursing over a gorgeous, bubbling track that fuses native instruments with electronic ones.

The motherhood sisterhood is my twenty-first-century consciousness-raising support group/rock band/writing circle. Come on girls, bring the noise.

I blame Tipper Gore for giving mothers a bad name during the '80s. Along with Republican wife Susan Baker, she—a former drummer herself—formed the Parents Music Resource Center. They successfully coerced the record industry into putting warning labels on albums with adult material. It was an annoying act of prudish motherly concern, just the kind of unhip conservatism I never wanted to fall into. Not that I don't wince when my girls relish songs about hustling nookie or cocaine. But I know if I tell them not to listen, they're just going to love those songs even more.

I don't want to become the aging boomer drummer who's stopped marching to a different beat. I've talked to pop critics, male and female, who complain they can't keep up with the crap kids are listening to these days, that they don't want to. I'm not going quietly into that twilight. I'm not saying I download iTunes with the zeal of a teenager or club like a twenty-two-year-old. But I haven't taken up a relationship with the oeuvres of Lawrence Welk, Basia, or Yanni either.

Three of my favorite CDs of the past couple years celebrate underclass revolution (M.I.A.'s *Arular*), pussy and marijuana (Brazilian Girls), and having a forty-ounce bottle of malt liquor in the morning (Morning 40 Federation's *Ticonderoga*). Stylistically, those CDs represent hip-hop, drum and bass, dancehall, grime, tango, trance, dub, punk, minstrel tunes, brass band music, and, hopefully, the future.

I did trade in my Mustang convertible for a PT Cruiser. We needed at least one vehicle the whole family could fit into—not that, four months later, we'd ever all ridden in it together. I've come to accept that our mismatched unit will never be the Brady Bunch, that if the girls sit down with Bud, Cole, and me for dinner, it's a minor miracle. Karlie and Kenda hate the Cruiser, even though I keep telling them that it is, literally, gangster: like a ride Bonnie and Clyde would have driven.

Mom, on the other hand, is thinking of getting a Cruiser herself.

We become our parents, the cliché says. I used to think that would be the end of the world. Now, when Cole turns to me and says a word that vibrates with childhood memories and that the king of rock 'n' roll himself deemed "all right"—"Mama"—I can't think of a greater honor.

Sitting on her kitchen floor with Wyatt, Kristin Hersh didn't look uninspired. "As soon as you have a kid, your place in the universe becomes fixed," she told me. "You know that you're there for someone else. That's a very freeing and productive position. And the rewards are not burdening ones; they're lightening. You feel like you can fly when you make these people."

I was wrong. In the course of writing this book, forgotten childhood memories returned. They hadn't been so much suppressed as supplanted over the years, as adventure overshadowed domestic bliss in my life's wanderings. They are memories of fantasies, of what happened after I saved Michael—or whomever—from the bullet and we pledged our love. "Turn around, and you're a mom." Children laughed and cuddled in the future of my dreams. Sometimes I couldn't hear them over the music, but they were there.

Acknowledgments

I have amazing family members and friends who were patient, kind, and generous in allowing me to write them into the story of my life. A book may not be better than a baby, but it's pretty damn good. In particular, thanks to Bud, for putting up with my endless brain working and for the subtitle. To Cole, Kenda, and Karlie, for making *Mamarama* possible. To Mom, for inspiration. To Dad, the best bridge partner ever. To Brett and Paul, true brothers of the sisterhood. To Bettie Lou, Babette, Peggy, and Bob: Thanks for letting me into the family.

To Sarah Lazin, not just an agent but an inspiration. To Alexis Rizzuto, for getting it. To Marnie Cochran, for also getting it. To Melissa Irgens, for spreading the words, and to Erin Sprague, for keeping them in order. To Georgia Liebman, for the wonderful cover.

To Susie J. Horgan, thanks for inspiring the title, reading the damn uncollated manuscript, and being a great friend. To Katherine Stewart, for line editing above and beyond the call of duty; so glad you're in my life. To the other Fictionaires, Jana Martin and Vivien Goldman, for years of help along the way. To Michelle Belleville, way-cool website designer and road buddy. To Vickie Starr, Cathay Che, Dina Suggs, Debbi Gibbs, Cara Buckley, Laura Quinlan, Maggie Steber, Lili Lorenzo, Cindy Pederson, Wanda Raiford, Silver Tyler, Brian Parks, and Ray Rogers: My friends are my life. To Sandy Murphy, for being mama to Cole's best friend and taking them both when I couldn't.

To Mike Tyler, for always being on my team and encouraging me to write this. To Mitchell Kaplan, for helping me figure out what I want to do.

To the cool, smart, strong, sexy women of my listening club and my book club.

To the *Miami Herald*, for giving me time to write this. Especially to Shelley Acoca, bestest boss and fellow Dairy Queen, and Carlos Mielgo, the numbers guy with the big heart.

To Rosa, Lucy, and Martha, without whose help *Mamarama* wouldn't have been possible.

To the future in children's eyes.

Credits

Diligent efforts have been made to contact copyright holders; please excuse any inadvertent errors or omissions, but if anyone has been unintentionally omitted, the publisher would be pleased to receive notification and to make acknowledgments in future printings.

All Rights Controlled and Administered by
EMI BLACKWOOD MUSIC INC.
All Rights Reserved. International Copyright Secured. Used by Permission.

Unpretty
Words and Music by Dallas Austin and Tionne Watkins
© 1999 EMI BLACKWOOD MUSIC INC., CYPTRON MUSIC,
EMI APRIL MUSIC INC. and GRUNGE GIRL MUSIC
All Rights for CYPTRON MUSIC Controlled and Administered by
EMI BLACKWOOD MUSIC INC.
All Rights for GRUNGE GIRL MUSIC Controlled and Administered
by EMI APRIL MUSIC INC.
All Rights Reserved. International Copyright Secured. Used by Permission.

Milkshake
Words by Pharrell Williams and Chad Hugo
Music by Pharrell Williams
© 2003 EMI BLACKWOOD MUSIC INC., WATERS OF
NAZARETH, CAREERS-BMG MUSIC PUBLISHING and
RAYNCHASER MUSIC
All Rights for WATERS OF NAZARETH Controlled and Administered
by EMI BLACKWOOD MUSIC INC.
All Rights for RAYNCHASER MUSIC Administered by
CAREERS-BMG MUSIC PUBLISHING
All Rights Reserved. International Copyright Secured. Used by Permission.

Dirt Off Your Shoulder
Words and Music by Shawn Carter and Tim Mosely © 2003 CARTER
BOYS PUBLISHING, VIRGINIA BEACH MUSIC, ZOMBA SONGS,

PANCAKEY CAKES MUSIC, KENJI KOBAYASHI MUSIC, BIG BAD
MR. HAHN MUSIC, NONDISCLOSURE AGREEMENT MUSIC,
ROB BOURDON MUSIC,
CHESTERCHAZ PUBLISHING, and WB MUSIC CORP.
All Rights for CARTER BOYS PUBLISHING Controlled and
Administered by EMI APRIL MUSIC INC.
All Rights PANCAKEY CAKES MUSIC, KENJI KOBAYASHI
MUSIC, BIG BAD MR. HAHN MUSIC, NONDISCLOSURE
AGREEMENT MUSIC, ROB BOURDON MUSIC and
CHESTERCHAZ PUBLISHING
Administered by ZOMBA SONGS
Lyrics Reprinted by Permission of ALFRED PUBLISHING CO., INC.
All Rights Reserved. International Copyright Secured. Used by Permission.

50 Foot Queenie
Words and Music by Polly Jean Harvey
© 1993 HOT HEAD MUSIC LTD. and EMI MUSIC PUBLISHING
LTD.
All Rights in the USA and Canada Controlled and Administered by
EMI BLACKWOOD MUSIC INC.
All Rights Reserved. International Copyright Secured. Used by Permission.

Turn Around
Words and Music by Alan Greene, Malvina Reynolds
and Harry Belafonte
Copyright © 1958; Renewed 1986 Alan Greene Songs (ASCAP) and
Clara Music Publishing Corp. (ASCAP)
Worldwide Rights for Alan Greene Songs Administered by Cherry Lane
Music Publishing Company, Inc.